GETTING
YOUR MESSAGE
ACROSS

*To the memory of Danton and Pollux —
with thanks for sharing your unparalleled wisdom
and insight*

GETTING
YOUR MESSAGE
ACROSS

THE SEVEN STEPS TO
COMMUNICATING SUCCESSFULLY
IN EVERY SITUATION

JAMES HOOKE & JEREMY PHILIPS

SIMON & SCHUSTER

AUSTRALIA

GETTING YOUR MESSAGE ACROSS

First published in Australasia in 1996 by
Simon & Schuster Australia
20 Barcoo Street, East Roseville NSW 2069

Viacom International
Sydney New York London Toronto Tokyo Singapore

© James Hooke and Jeremy Philips 1996

The Publishers would like to point out that every effort has been made
to contact the copyright holders of extracts included in *Getting Your
Message Across*. They would be pleased to hear from anyone who has
not been duly acknowledged.

National Library of Australia
Cataloguing-in-Publication data

Hooke, James, 1970 – .
Getting your message across : the seven steps to
communicating successfully in every situation.

ISBN 0 7318 0550 X.

1. Oral communication. 2. Public speaking.
I. Philips, Jeremy, 1972 – . II. Title.

808.5

Cover designed by Michael Killalea
Designed and typeset by Joy Eckermann
Printed in Australia by Griffin Paperbacks

ACKNOWLEDGEMENTS

There were many people who assisted in the production of this book and we are grateful to them all. Below we have singled out a few to whom we would like to show our particular appreciation.

We must, of course, thank our respective families. It was our families who convinced us, albeit inadvertently, of the desperate need for a book on how to communicate more effectively. Further, we are grateful to them for doing little to impede the writing process.

Thanks also to Peter Freeman, editor of the Opinion Section at the *Australian Financial Review*. He gave us the initial opportunity to get our message across on his pages and stood by us in the face of numerous Letters to the Editor which disagreed with every opinion we proffered.

We would like to thank John Sheldon of Sydney Grammar School who first set us on the path to effective communication. He understood that communication skills needed to be actively taught and not just learnt by osmosis.

We shall always be indebted to the University of New South Wales, particularly Vice-Chancellor Professor John Niland. The University gave us enormous assistance, most notably in attending the World Debating Championship, and has been a great source of encouragement.

Our greatest thanks go to Simon & Schuster. Susan Morris-Yates showed tremendous faith in us from the outset. We enjoyed working with her enormously, especially during the robust contractual negotiations phase. Her suggestions and encouragement were crucial to the end product.

Other people at Simon & Schuster went the distance. Brigitta Doyle is a very patient editor. We give her thanks, particularly for the sections that she convinced us to delete.

We would particularly like to thank Rick Kalowski whose support and advice in this venture was, as always, tremendous. His comments on the draft manuscript were insightful and constructive, and helped us correct some of our worst excesses.

Thanks also to Timothy Hughes who was kind enough to read and critique the draft manuscript, which was of great help. Tim's judgment and advice is always an asset.

Thanks to Sascha Kelso for the illustrations that appear in Chapter Four. Her creativity in the face of vague instructions was wonderful.

Jeremy also gives special thanks to Tracy J. Francis whose geographic absence gave him more time to write, and whose support was not diminished by distance.

CONTENTS

INTRODUCTION

When asked to list great leaders, many of us cite those who were excellent communicators: Winston Churchill, John F. Kennedy, Martin Luther King. Many figures from political history have become great leaders in our minds as much for their skill as communicators as for the quality of their management and policies. When we remember these great leaders, it is often their words that come to mind rather than their great deeds — 'We shall fight them on the beaches'; 'Ask not what your country can do for you, but what you can do for your country' and, of course, 'I have a dream . . .'.

But it is not just great leaders who must deliver important speeches. At certain times in our lives we are all called upon to speak to signify the importance of the occasion — weddings, funerals, the few well-chosen words at a friend's birthday. Significant moments in a social context are often heralded by an audience calling 'Speech, speech, speech!'.

While some people take advantage of any and every opportunity to speak, others shy away from such invitations. Yet no matter how daunting we may find the prospect of addressing an audience of more than one, we all know that on some occasion we will have no choice. At some stage we all have to face our fear and speak in front of an audience.

What is effective communication?

Effective communication is a matter of getting your message across successfully. You have succeeded when you have used communication to achieve your desired goal.

Effective communication does not have to be flashy or verbose. A successful speech does not have to bring tears to the eyes of all who hear it. All that is necessary is that the speaker's message is successfully transmitted to the audience. The ability to inspire tears or laughter may be a great skill but it is not a prerequisite for effective communication.

There are many examples of expert communicators in our society. Advertising agencies, for instance, employ experts in communicating a message. But there is no *one* most effective way to communicate. In advertising, there are many ways to convey the message: some ads are funny, others are serious; some have many images, others are more simple. To be effective, an advertisement must satisfy only one requirement: it must sell the product by getting the message across. The same is true of effective communication.

Why effective communication is important

The spoken word is a powerful tool. It can be used for good: to prevent war, to express love, to entertain, or to inspire. It can also be used for harm: to deceive, to arouse hatred, to generate conflict. Whatever the purpose, plainly the spoken word is powerful. Those who have mastered oral communication are able to harness that power.

According to the popular children's rhyme: 'Sticks and stones will break my bones, but words will never hurt me.' As much as we try to persuade children of the truth of this principle, we all know how upsetting the spoken word can be. Similarly, we all know how wonderful and moving it can be.

Most of us understand our limitations — 'I get nervous', 'I'm not a funny person' — but believe that we can communicate satisfactorily in most situations. It is only when 'words fail us' that we become frustrated by our inability to put our thoughts into words.

While most people can communicate *satisfactorily*, few can communicate *effectively*. Given that the spoken word is so powerful, as a society we are increasingly coming to realise how important it is to be able to get our messages across. As the world becomes more competitive, as jobs become more scarce, and as the communication age takes hold, it is becoming clear that being able to communicate satisfactorily is not enough.

Most people realise that communication is important. In both personal and professional life the ability to communicate well can make the difference between success and failure.

When you meet someone for the first time, your first impression of them will largely be based on how well they communicate. If their manner of speech is nervous or boring then you will assume that *they* are nervous and boring. While we all know that it is important to make a good first impression, not everyone has mastered the necessary skills.

Effective communication is also essential in a work environment. Employees who can communicate effectively will be promoted faster and will be more successful — whether making client presentations or communicating their ideas to the boss. In some instances an employer may be prepared to put up with someone who has difficulty communicating but this person will not be promoted as far or as rapidly as they might have been had they mastered the skills of successful communication.

Even getting a job depends upon the ability to communicate effectively. Most job interviews are, in reality, a test of how well you communicate. The interviewer already knows from your résumé what you look like on paper. The interview is an opportunity for the interviewer to assess you in person. If you communicate effectively and answer and ask questions well, then you will create a good impression. The interviewer will naturally assume that you are an intelligent, motivated person. The next candidate may actually be better suited to the job than you, but if they are unable to communicate this to the interviewer they are unlikely to be given an opportunity to demonstrate their prowess.

Every day we experience situations where we want to persuade someone of our point of view, inspire someone to action, or inform someone of a fact. Whether talking our way out of a parking fine or requesting a pay rise, there are always times that we would like to be particularly persuasive.

In this book we focus on communicating effectively in *every* situation. Not just a speech to twenty million television viewers, but also the one-to-one communication which occurs every day of our lives.

Effective communication can be learnt

Many people view the ability to communicate effectively as some form of birthright. The expression 'You've either got it or you ain't' is often used in relation to communication skills. The false perception is that these skills are inherited rather than learnt and that speakers are effective, not because they work at it, but because they are lucky.

Nothing could be further from the truth. While some people are naturally better speakers than others, anyone can learn to be an effective communicator.

We all know the basics of speaking, but there are many communication skills that must be learnt. For instance, few people know how to use eye contact when speaking to an audience of five hundred. While this is an easy skill to learn, it is not one that people possess inherently. Fortunately, it can be taught easily — we cover this in Chapter Four.

Perhaps the greatest advantage of learning to

communicate effectively is increased confidence. Most people are terrified by the prospect of having to give a speech, whether in a professional or a social setting. The first step to overcoming nervousness is to learn the basics of effective communication. If you know what you are doing you will be more confident. While there are specific techniques that can be used to overcome nervousness (see Chapter Two), learning how to communicate effectively is the most important step in conquering fear.

About this book

Getting Your Message Across is designed to help you develop an ability to communicate effectively in every situation. Each step to successful communication is important. Plainly, we all have different strengths and weaknesses. The challenge is to build on your strengths and work on your weaknesses.

Getting Your Message Across sets out the seven steps to effective communication. By working through each chapter, step-by-step, you too will be able to speak confidently and with ease.

CHAPTER ONE

FOCUS ON THE PRECISE OBJECTIVE

In a war . . . let your great object be victory, not lengthy campaigns
SUN TZU, *THE ART OF WAR*

The importance of determining your objective before you undertake a task must not be underestimated. 'Know your goal' has become a cliché because it is sound advice.

An example of the need for a focused objective can be seen in the world of house-hunting. You could go about buying a house by announcing to a real estate agent: 'I want to buy a new home. I don't know where, how much I want to pay or what type of home I want, but I want a new home.' Plainly, however, a more focused approach will be more effective. Before meeting an agent, you focus on what type of new home you want — how many bedrooms, what suburb, how much you want to pay. By taking this second approach, you save yourself (and the real estate agent) time and ensure that you are more likely to buy the house you want than the house the agent wants for you.

Before speaking, you should always determine the precise objective of your communication — you should not set out on any journey until you know where you are headed.

In many instances of communication, the precise objective is predetermined. In these cases, you know the precise objective because it has been explicitly stated or it is implicit in the context of the communication. For instance, when the defence council in a murder trial makes her closing address to the jury, the precise objective is clear: to obtain a 'not guilty' verdict.

Sometimes, however, the precise objective of the communication is less clear. When the objective has not been predetermined, you must spend time analysing the context of the communication to determine your precise objective. For instance, if you are asked to deliver a speech to the annual meeting of the National Asthma Foundation, the precise objective of your speech may not be immediately apparent. Do the organisers want a witty after dinner speech or a complex technical presentation? As the speaker, you will have to determine your precise objective: is it to inform, to persuade, to entertain or to inspire?

Without meaning to upset any animal liberationists, there are many ways to skin a cat. However, before you commence skinning, you should make the conscious decision that a skinned cat is what you actually want. So too with communication.

For instance, there are numerous ways of persuading someone that gravity exists — you can shout it at them, show them a textbook, or drop a textbook from a building. But before choosing which method of persuasion to adopt, you must first decide that persuading your friend of the existence of gravity is what you want to do.

In this chapter, we discuss the importance of determining the precise objective that you hope to achieve from the communication before you even open your mouth. To use communication to help achieve your goals you must first have isolated those goals. What you say and how you say it will depend on your objectives.

The second concept that we deal with in this chapter is how to identify the precise objective before you speak. It is all well and good to know that you must identify your goals, but knowing this is useless if you do not know *how* to identify them.

Communication is a means to an end, and this chapter discusses methods for making it easier for you to view your goal clearly. The more precisely you can visualise the target, the easier it is to take aim.

THE IMPORTANCE OF IDENTIFYING YOUR OBJECTIVE

Communicating without a clearly defined objective is like turning up at the airport and trying to buy a plane ticket without knowing your destination: if you really can't decide where to go, stay at home. Similarly, if you can't work out what your communication objective is, perhaps you would be better off saying nothing.

Don't neglect your objectives

If you fail to focus on your objectives you run two risks:

1. **The communication meanders**. Often the communication fails to accomplish anything. For instance, someone calls a meeting but when everyone arrives no one is quite sure why they are there. This frequently results in a meandering discussion that may fill in the time allocated but makes no real progress. Another example is a toast at a wedding. Often the speaker has no clear idea as to the purpose of the exercise — how funny to be, how formal to be, how long to speak for, what to talk about. The toast just rambles along without anyone quite understanding what its purpose is.

2. **The communication is hijacked**. The second risk if you are not focused on your objective is that your communication can be 'hijacked'. Others can divert discussion to suit their own purpose and prevent you addressing your agenda. For instance, if you attend a parents' meeting at your child's school without knowing

what you want to discuss, other more determined (or more confident) parents may hijack the discussion to discuss issues of relevance to them but not to you.

Having a clear sense of purpose and using your 'air time' to its best advantage to accomplish that purpose will ensure your communication is effective.

HOW TO DEFINE YOUR OBJECTIVES
What does success look like?

Too many people step headlong into the fray without first pausing to ask themselves a crucial question:

> What does success look like?

In some cases a successful outcome will be that everybody laughs a lot and is very entertained. In other cases, success will mean that you are offered the job you were after, that the board accepts your recommendation to build a new plant, or that you get a full cash refund for that faulty toaster.

Success is the achievement of your objectives. If the shop assistant empathises with you about the toaster but refuses to give you a refund, you have failed. On the other hand, sometimes empathy will be all you want; for instance, if you are complaining about your life to a friend.

Sometimes understanding the purpose of your communication will be quite straightforward. If you are being interviewed for a job, for instance, the purpose is fairly plain: you want to convince your interviewer that you are the best person for the job. You may also have a subsidiary purpose: to find out more about the company and the job so that you can decide whether it is really what you want.

In other cases, however, determining the purpose of

your communication will not be so easy. If you are invited to give a speech on a particular topic to a group of people whom you don't know, you need to be careful to define, clearly, what it is that you are trying to accomplish.

What do you want the audience to take away?

Before you start to speak, you should always consider how you wish your audience to see you. For instance, some people often use an angry tone when communicating. If you are frustrated, this may make you feel better, but it will rarely help you to achieve your objective. Although it may seem obvious, anger is an appropriate tool only when your objective is to show someone how angry you are. If you want better service in a restaurant or an apology from someone, then anger may not be the best way to get what you want.

It is crucial that you have decided what you want the audience to think of you before you begin communicating. People who define their objectives too vaguely can get trapped in a kind of 'no man's land', and suffer accordingly.

Be specific about your objective

Usually your objective for any communication is to have your audience do something, know something, feel something or hold a certain opinion. You may want a committee to adopt your proposal, your students to learn about a particular subject, your partner to marry you, or to be elected to office. Being specific about your precise objective and what you want to achieve makes it easier to work out the best way of getting there. You need to view your objective through a telephoto lens rather than pointing to the horizon generally and saying 'I want to take a photo somewhere in that direction'.

An example of how being specific about your

objectives can affect the way you go about reaching your goals can be seen in the world of sport. At the start of each football season, a coach must determine the team's objective. Some coaches set ambitious targets such as, 'To win all our games', whereas others say, 'To win the championship'. Both of these objectives are lofty but they are *not* the same.

Winning the championship at the end of the season may mean building the team up to peak performance at the right time. Similarly, it may mean resting some players for less important games so they can overcome injury. The objective of winning every game is not the same. The coach may not be able to rest players if winning each game is the objective. While these two objectives may overlap, and may sometimes lead to the same result, they are not identical.

The importance of defining the precise objective can also be illustrated by the following example of a debate in the World Debating Championship. The debate was before an audience of about four hundred people on the subject 'That the letter of the law is more important than the spirit of the law'. Our objective was precise: to persuade a majority of the five judges that we had won the debate. Our opponents' objective appeared to be slightly different: to demonstrate that they were smarter than us. Although these objectives may appear to be similar, they're really quite different. It was theoretically possible for both teams to achieve their objectives.

Our exceedingly confident opponents commenced speaking in favour of the letter of the law by explaining how as yuppie lawyers in London, there was nothing more frustrating to them than judges ignoring the letter of one particular tax law in favour of its spirit. Under the letter of the law a new BMW may be tax deductible as 'industry transport equipment', but judges rejected such deductions for being contrary to the spirit of that same law. Their point was that if the legislature didn't want BMWs to be tax deductible, then the law should be changed by parliament, not by judges.

Our opponent's example was valid but foolish. Defending BMW–driving, tax-evading yuppie lawyers was unlikely to endear them to the audience (unless the audience happened to be full of kindred spirits), even though the example may have had some technical merit.

Our response was to make humorous but derogatory comments about BMW–driving, tax-evading yuppie lawyers from London. Fortuitously for us, our opponents were the only members of this demographic in the audience. As it was, we also won the intellectual argument. But we could have won the debate merely by undermining our opponents' credibility and showing that they were on the side of the rich and privileged while we stood for justice for all.

The point of this example is that often people say something which is technically correct, factually true, or historically accurate, but which casts them in a negative light. If you have not first defined your objectives accurately and precisely, your selection of technically correct material may yet hinder your cause.

Similarly, as a candidate for political office, you may know some very funny jokes of an adult nature. If you were to tell these jokes, an audience may think that you are a funny person. But that same audience may also decide that you are unfit for the office for which you are campaigning (though possibly not!). Having the audience like you and think that you're funny will not always help you to reach your goal. You must precisely define your objectives to avoid these traps.

Even when your goal seems predetermined — for instance, you want the Board of Directors to accept your proposal — you need to define your *precise* objective. Do you have to persuade every member of the audience, half of the audience, or only certain key members of the audience? The more precisely you define your objective, the better you can tailor your message to achieve that objective.

Purpose of the message

How you want to affect your audience will be fundamental to the approach you adopt. You need decide whether you want to persuade, inform, inspire, entertain or achieve some combination of these reactions.

To persuade — the 'we should do this' speech

The most common objective of communication is to persuade. You want your audience to accept a certain proposition that you are putting to them.

The art of persuasion can be quite subtle. You need to be quite specific about what you are proposing and who exactly you are trying to persuade. If you are seeking preselection for a seat in parliament, your objective will probably be to convince more than half of the preselectors that you are the best candidate. Given the choice, you would prefer 55 per cent of the preselectors to support you and 45 per cent to oppose you, rather than all the preselectors to feel indifferent towards you.

In this instance, you may be willing to alienate some members of your audience to win over others because you know that if you try to please everyone you will end up with no one on your side.

In other cases, however, consensus may be more important. If you are being interviewed for a job by a panel of five people, you will want to make sure that no one is against you. One veto could be fatal. Here your minimum objective is to try to foster at least one or two strong supporters on the panel while making sure that the other members are at least reasonably well-disposed towards you. This is preferable to having three members supporting you but two vehemently opposed to you.

Exhibit 1.1 *Focus on the precise objective*

Principle	This	Not this
Determine your objective before acting	My objective is to buy a new two-bedroom flat in the city centre for no more than $200,000	My objective is to visit a real estate agent and see what is for sale because I want a new flat
Do not confuse the objective with the process	My objective is to be offered the job I want at $60,000	My objective is to describe my skills and background and why I want to work for this company
Be specific rather than general about your objective	My objective is to persuade the Board that we need to start selling a new product (crushed ice) into a new market (the Antarctic)	My objective is to explain why we need to diversify
	My objective is to convince my spouse to come with me to Hawaii for two weeks	My objective is to convince my spouse that it is time we took a holiday

To inform — the 'how to use your lawnmower' speech

Sometimes your objective will be to inform, to present the facts, rather than to persuade your audience of any particular point of view. In this case you should be careful to avoid becoming argumentative.

Often an audience finds it difficult to distinguish between a presentation of empirical facts and an argument where you are putting forward a particular point of view. If you are intending merely to present the facts, don't defend a particular point of view and try to avoid entering into a debate about the conclusions to be drawn from the facts.

The danger in this situation is that you can be drawn into a debate that you never intended to enter, and can end up supporting a proposition which you had not given much thought to in advance.

There is often a tendency for an audience to hold you responsible when you present unexpected bad news, but you can reduce the likelihood of this occurring if you just present the facts, without commentary or conclusions. There is a big difference between a presentation that shows that if the company continues at its current 'run rate' it will be bankrupt by the end of the year, and one that lays blame for the parlous state of the company's finances on a particular person or group within the company. Seldom will vindictiveness and the allocation of blame be effective tools of communication.

When giving a purely fact-based presentation you need to make sure you let the audience know from the outset that this is what you're doing. You also need to be prepared for the obvious 'So what do you think we should do about this?' question at the end. If you are not able to give a spontaneous answer then you need to have a satisfactory answer prepared, one which proposes some steps which may be taken to solve the relevant problem. (See Chapter Six for more information on questions and answers.)

To inspire — the 'carpe diem' speech

Carpe diem is a Latin phrase that means 'seize the day'. It was popularised by the American poet Walt Whitman. The phrase and the sentiment were subsequently used as the basis for the film *Dead Poets Society*.

Some people are looking for inspiration from a communication. They will respond well to 'I have a dream' speeches, short on facts and specifics, but long on vision. These are speeches that try to rouse the audience and impress upon them the need to do something. *Carpe diem* speeches touch the hearts of the audience more than their minds.

There are some truly memorable examples of this type of speech. Dictionaries of quotations and collections of speeches tend to be full of this type of material. Martin Luther King, Winston Churchill and John F. Kennedy were particularly good at this style of speech. An excellent example of this style is a speech by Theodore Roosevelt before the Hamilton Club in Chicago on 10 April 1899:

> Far better it is to dare mighty things, to win glorious triumphs, even though checkered by failure, than to take rank with those poor spirits who neither enjoy much nor suffer much, because they live in the grey twilight that knows no victory nor defeat.

Inspirational speeches are often confused with speeches that have the primary objective of persuading. While the two have some similarities, there are some crucial differences. The objective when persuading someone is more cerebral and less emotional than when seeking to inspire. When inspiring, style is far more crucial than it is when persuading. Some of the great inspirational speeches of history have been almost bereft of what would traditionally be referred to as substance.

You should only include inspiration as one of your precise objectives of communication when you feel confident that you will be able to inspire the audience effectively. Yet even nervous and hesitant people can overcome their disposition and give inspirational speeches.

To entertain — the 'horse walks into a bar' routine

Sometimes the purpose of your communication will be to entertain the audience. While your speech or story may have a message, the primary focus is entertainment. An example of this is when you tell a humorous story, such as: 'A horse walks into a bar and the barman says, "Why the long face?" '.

This is a very difficult form of communication. For it to work well, it must look as though it comes naturally and spontaneously. It need not *actually* come naturally, but it must *appear* as though it does. Before singling humour out as an objective, consider carefully if you have the confidence to carry it through. This form of communication is inherently difficult for most people — we provide some advice on making communication more entertaining in Chapter Four.

KEY POINTS

The importance of defining your objective

- Communication without a clear objective is likely to meander aimlessly and accomplish little

Define your objective

- Picture what success looks like
- Be specific rather than general about your objectives
- Don't confuse the process — how to reach your goal — with the objective — what you want to achieve with the communication

Be clear about the nature of your message

- *Persuade*: clearly determine whom you want to persuade; often there are only a few key decision-makers
- *Inform*: distinguish between the presentation of facts and a point of view; if you intend only to present uncontroversial facts, then don't become involved in arguments or exchanges of opinion
- *Inspire*: in this type of communication style is usually more important than substance — you need to be able to deliver more than a convincing argument to inspire the audience
- *Entertain:* you must appear to be natural and spontaneous to succeed if telling humorous stories or jokes

CHAPTER TWO

PREPARE FOR THE COMMUNICATION

Skill without imagination is craftsmanship . . .
Imagination without skill give us modern art
TOM STOPPARD

When preparing for competition, every successful sporting great does a huge amount of practice, whether it's swimming laps of the pool, running around the oval, pumping weights or practising their ball skills. Why? Because, according to the world's most irritating cliché, *practice makes perfect*. While we cannot dispute this, there is more to preparation than just practice. For instance, athletes also need to learn and master the rules of the game and learn about their opponent and study his moves.

Communication is not all that different. While practice builds confidence, there are specific steps you should take to prepare for any communication.

To be a successful athlete you must prepare for competition. To be a successful student you need to prepare for exams. So too with communication. Preparation is *crucial*.

When it comes to communication, many people view preparation as unnecessary. They believe that, because they have been speaking all their lives, there is nothing to it, or that to communicate well you simply open your mouth and let the words spill out. For some this may be true (although we've never met them!), but for most this is an illusion. While you may not make a fool of yourself if you fail to prepare, you will find that preparation improves your effectiveness.

You may not get fired if you don't prepare for meetings, but you may get promoted if you do. Similarly, you may be elected to the your local community safety committee without preparing a nomination speech, but you are more likely to be elected president of the committee if you do.

When we refer to preparation in this chapter, we are referring to the background preparation that needs to be done *before* you communicate. This includes such elements as knowing and understanding your audience, and preparing appropriate content and style.

We have divided this chapter into the two stages of preparation that we recommend — knowing the audience, and planning content and style. Whether you are giving a speech at a wedding, attending a job interview or going to a meeting at work, the same basic principles apply in relation to preparation.

PART A: KNOW YOUR AUDIENCE

In any communication the audience is the person or people you are speaking to, both directly and indirectly. In a social conversation, the audience consists of those who are listening to you and contributing to the conversation. In a business meeting, the audience consists of those present at the meeting, as well as anyone else who might later read a report of the proceedings. In a radio interview, the immediate audience is the person who is asking you the questions but the indirect audience is obviously much larger.

Successful communication involves understanding who makes up the audience. You can only prepare for your communication if you know the audience — what they will like, how they will react, what they believe in. If you are speaking to the Association of Animal Liberationists, for instance, you will be hard pressed to sell the concept of 'Hunting Holidays'.

There are four steps you should take when researching the audience:

1. Find out who they are
2. Work out who the *real* audience is
3. Assess the context of the communication
4. Discover what the audience needs.

Who are they?

Different audiences have different sensitivities. These sensitivities may have to do with the audience's sex, age, ethnic background, sexual preference, religion, occupation, and numerous other factors. Not only must you be sensitive to your audience while you speak, but you must keep them in mind when preparing for your communication.

The more you know about your audience, the better. The more information you have about them, the better you can tailor your communication to them and so improve its effectiveness.

For instance, if you know that most of the people you will be speaking to are involved in finance, then a detailed financial explanation may be appropriate. However, if you will be speaking to a group of plumbers, the same financial analysis might simply inspire them to glaze over or fall asleep.

Some of the methods you can use to identify the audience include:

• asking the host or organiser what type of people will be attending
• asking an audience member if they know who will be attending

- arriving at the venue before you are due to speak and meeting as many members of the audience as possible.

You also need to think about what effect your words will have on your audience. Don't just think about your position, think about theirs. At a job interview, for instance, try to imagine what your interviewer (who will probably be your boss if you get the job) has at stake. She is probably wondering whether you will help make her department more productive, and how you would fit in. You need to try to focus on her issues.

In other cases, your communication may have unintended ramifications. For instance, you may make a suggestion in a meeting at work that will jeopardise a colleague's position or undermine her credibility. Conversely, some of your colleagues may benefit from your proposal if it is adopted. You need to consider, in advance, how they will gain or lose if your proposal is accepted.

Who is the *real* audience?

The *real* audience consists of those people you must influence in order to achieve your objectives. Sometimes the real audience will be a subset of the whole audience in the room. At other times the real audience will not even be present when you speak. Your communication may be recorded on tape, video or in note form by a member of the audience to be repeated or reported on at a later date.

Similarly, in one-to-one communication, the audience is not always as it appears. If you are communicating by telephone with someone's secretary and are impatient and rude when leaving a message, this information may be conveyed to your real audience — the person you wish to speak to.

No matter what the situation, you must determine whom you actually wish to influence. This will affect how you prepare the communication.

When the real audience is a subset of the actual audience

There will be occasions when influencing everyone who is listening to you is not your main concern. There may be thirty people at a meeting, only one of whom makes the final decision. Similarly, there may be three thousand delegates at a convention, only fifty of whom have voting rights. In each case the person that you seek to influence is the person with the vote. While it may be an added bonus if everyone else is persuaded, that is not necessary for you to achieve your objective. A precise objective would be: to persuade those who are currently undecided without losing any existing support.

Politicians fully understand this principle. At election time, political parties target their advertising at a specific group of people within the electorate. In their case, the target audience is undecided voters. There is no point in preaching to the converted (though they should not be taken for granted). Similarly, there is no point in preaching to the unconvertible. Once a political party realises this, they direct their advertising carefully. To them, the real audience is only about 20 per cent of the total electorate.

While your precise objective may be to persuade a specific audience member, it is important in this situation not to single out the individual when you are speaking. It is somewhat disconcerting for the audience if, instead of addressing everyone at a meeting, you stare at the managing director simply because she is the one who will decide the issue.

When the real audience is not present

When the real audience is not present in the actual audience, your task becomes more difficult.

We all know of situations in which a conversation has been subsequently misreported. The children's game 'Chinese Whispers' shows just how distorted messages can become when they are repeated by others. If you know that your communication will only reach the real audience through other people, then keep it as simple and logical as possible. The clearer you are, the more likely it is that the message will be accurately repeated.

This has ramifications when preparing for the communication. When your real audience is not present, you should not try to achieve too much. The possible objectives are limited by the way the message will reach the *real* audience. The more complex your message, the greater the likelihood that it will be misreported when it is repeated to a third party. If you know that someone is summarising what you are saying to relay to someone else, you should make their task as easy as possible. This necessarily limits what you can hope to achieve from the communication.

It is always preferable, if you can, to engineer it so that you present the material to your real audience yourself. If that's not possible, then the next best thing is to make sure that the message gets through clearly to those who will be carrying the torch.

For instance, you may have to give a presentation to some senior executives about how much capital expenditure will be required to undertake a new project. While this audience is important, the real audience that you should have in mind is the Board of Directors, as they will ultimately decide whether or not to allocate the capital. So you will need to be mindful of how your message will be carried by your audience to the Board.

In situations like this, there are always a number of concerns, not least being that your presentation may be butchered by the time that someone else presents it.

There are three main techniques that can be used to help avoid subsequent misrepresentation:

1. Prepare a one page summary of your message. This

'executive summary' will hopefully be presented to your audience intact.

2. Use signposting when speaking (see Chapter Four). This will make your message clearer and easier to summarise.

3. Repeat your key points to ensure that your 'messenger' clearly understands the message.

Understand the context of the communication

Understanding what stake your audience has in what you are saying is fundamental to preparing for communication.

First you need to think about why they are listening to you. Were they told to or did they voluntarily come at your invitation? Are they directly involved in the issue at stake? If you are making a proposal at work, who will be affected if your proposal is adopted?

Taking the time to understand these issues will help you decide how to position your communication and how to select the appropriate tone to adopt.

Second, you should analyse the context of the communication. This is done by considering the context from different perspectives. How formal is the setting? What is the history of the occasion? Will the communication be considered private or will it be quoted extensively? Will your performance reflect on other parties, such as your employer or your spouse, or only upon you?

There are an infinite number of factors that define the context of any communication. Thorough preparation requires that you consider these factors and tailor your communication accordingly.

What does your audience need?

If you find a group of people at a job centre, herd them all into a room and try to sell them Rolls Royces, you are unlikely to be successful. What they really need is a job.

In any communication you should be aware of the

need level of your audience. You should try to pitch your communication at a level that will connect with what they need or want. Ignoring what your audience needs is a common mistake, and one that can undermine the effectiveness of your communication.

Maslow's classic hierarchy of needs (see Exhibit 2.1) proposes that humans have different levels of need. Maslow's theory states that it is not until we have fulfilled our basic requirements that we begin to search for the next level of need. We do not proceed to level 2 until we have satisfied level 1.

For instance, if you are giving a talk to a group of

Exhibit 2.1 *Maslow's hierarchy of needs*

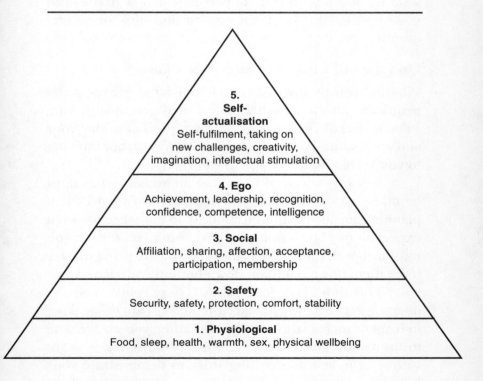

5.
Self-actualisation
Self-fulfilment, taking on
new challenges, creativity,
imagination, intellectual stimulation

4. Ego
Achievement, leadership, recognition,
confidence, competence, intelligence

3. Social
Affiliation, sharing, affection, acceptance,
participation, membership

2. Safety
Security, safety, protection, comfort, stability

1. Physiological
Food, sleep, health, warmth, sex, physical wellbeing

old-age pensioners about investing their superannuation, there is little point discussing long-term investments. They will not be interested in the possibility of huge returns on their money if they invest it for thirty years. It does not fit in with the hierarchy of their needs. Similarly, if you are talking to a group of highly paid executives, there is no point telling them how to save money on the bus fare. They just won't be interested.

At the same time, however, you can pitch your communication to the audience's aspirations. When seeking to inspire an audience with promises of future glory, it must be a future that they can actually visualise. The pot of gold at the end of the rainbow is only worth chasing if the audience ascribes a high value to gold. For instance, it will be difficult to persuade people of the need to save water if it has been raining non-stop for several months.

Understand what your audience wants

Whether you are giving a speech in front of five thousand people, making a presentation to a small group, or having a one-to-one discussion, you need to understand what your audience wants. Why are they there? Why are they listening to you? What do they hope to gain?

Any preconceived ideas that an audience has must be taken into account (if you are aware of them) when planning for the communication. If an audience has high expectations of how funny or interesting you will be, you must deal with those expectations. If you are going to have to let them down, let them down honestly but gently.

This should be done subtly. There is little point in opening a speech with, 'Unaccustomed as I am to speaking in front of such a large audience'. Rather, you may choose to disarm the audience by the use of humour, or begin with a light, self-deprecating story to demonstrate your humility.

Different audiences respond to different approaches

To communicate effectively you don't have to be a chameleon. You don't have to mould yourself to fit in with every person you communicate with. At the same time, however, you should be aware of what approach your audience might respond to best and modify your communication to take that into account. This doesn't mean dramatically altering your persona, it simply means that there are different aspects of your personality that you should use at different times, depending on the audience.

Do they like numbers?

In both professional and personal life, there are broadly two types of people: those who like and think in numbers and those who don't.

In some cases this distinction will be irrelevant. If you are speaking to a group of people about art criticism, for instance, numbers are probably not going to be relevant, whether the audience happens to like them or not. But in many other cases you will be able to make your point in a variety of ways. If you are speaking to a group of accountants, financiers or engineers, they are probably going to love numbers and technical charts and details. On the other hand, poets, actors or art teachers probably will not. Numbers will just make them switch off.

Sometimes this significantly affects what you can hope to achieve with the communication. If you are presenting complex numerical data — for instance, if you are teaching a navigation course to a group of recreational sailors — then you need to tailor your objectives to the audience. You may have to limit your precise objectives from the communication if you want the audience to keep up. Recreational sailors are unlikely to have a background in statistical analysis, so you need to keep numerical complexity to a minimum and explain difficult statistical concepts clearly and methodically. It is crucial that you take this into account when planning your presentation.

Are they 'touchy-feely'?

If you conjure up images of a family, warm and cosy in front of a fire, to try to reinforce a point, the audience's reaction will depend very much on their background. A group of bankers and computer programmers may be completely nonplussed. At the same time, counsellors and psychologists may find this image quite persuasive. They are more 'touchy-feely' and will respond well to the image of warmth and security.

You need to understand what type of message your audience will latch on to. When planning for the communication, you must assess the potential responsiveness of the audience to the type of subject matter that you are presenting. For instance, if you were to give a talk on safe sex to a university football team, you would expect some crass comments and a general air of levity. This not only affects the way that you present your material but, more fundamentally, it also has an impact on what you can hope to achieve when addressing such a group.

Are they looking for a bottom line?

When your audience consists of very busy, time-conscious people, conciseness is paramount. This type of audience will want a quick summary, the 'bottom line' and action steps.

While you should be prepared to delve into detail, you can often skip it unless the audience asks for it. This type of audience is probably not interested in the process behind the information or the detail underlying the main points. They want to know what it's going to cost and what they are going to gain.

When preparing for this form of communication, it is important that you neatly and succinctly summarise your ideas. Have the 'bottom line' ready for the audience. It is also useful to prepare three bullet point reasons as to why your bottom line is valid (see Chapter Three).

PART B: CONTENT AND STYLE

PREPARE THE CONTENT

Perhaps the most obvious aspect of preparation is selecting the content of your presentation. The importance of this cannot be overestimated — if you haven't thought about what you'd like to talk about, you may neglect to cover the key issues when the time comes to speak.

For instance, if you have to attend a parent–teacher meeting at your child's school, you should decide what you wish to talk about with the teacher in advance. If you wait until you arrive at the school before thinking about what you want to discuss, you are more likely to react to other people's issues than bring up the matters of most concern to you.

Be an expert

Plainly, it is a good idea to know what you are talking about. Being an expert doesn't mean that you have to be the world's leading authority on the material you are presenting. It does mean that you should be sufficiently familiar with the material and the relevant issues so that you can present yourself as authoritative and credible, and be able to deal with reasonable questions when they arise.

Often speakers get caught out by the most obvious gaps in knowledge. For instance, if you put up a chart that has an acronym on it, make sure you know what the acronym stands for. If you show that profit declined markedly in March, make sure you know why (or at least have some back-up data): did volumes decrease, did prices decrease or did costs increase? Similarly, if you are applying for a loan from your bank, the bank manager will expect you to be able to answer questions about your current expenditure and financial history. You will need to be prepared to explain the answers on your application form rather than just reiterate what you have written.

At the same time, you should be wary of pretending you know more than you do. If you don't know the answer to a question, it is unwise to bluster or make it up; someone will always see through you. The best approach is to say, 'Good question. I'll check on that and get straight back to you'.

The only thing worse than blustering is continually apologising or issuing massive disclaimers at the beginning of your speech. How many times have you seen someone start their presentation by saying, 'Well, I'm not really sure about what I'm presenting today because I've only had a few days to look at it, and of course you are all much more knowledgeable about this than I am, but here's what I've found'? Never look as if you are trying to cover your back by disclaimers. If you really have no idea, then you should not be speaking — it would obviously be a waste of time.

To be highly effective, you generally need to know more than just the basics. You need to have some depth and understanding of the issues you are presenting.

When making a presentation to colleagues or a group of managers, often you will show a dozen or so slides to illustrate the key points. As part of your preparation, you need to critically assess the material that you are presenting. Obvious questions for which you must have an answer include:

• where did that number come from?
• how did you calculate it?
• what assumptions have you made?

You need to be prepared to do more than just explain what is on your charts. When you give a presentation on a particular subject, your audience will assume that you have a degree of competence which is broader than the material that you present. If you are giving a presentation on why widget sales have declined, for instance, you need to know about more than sales data. Even if you have no intention of presenting any material about marketing, you will probably want to be familiar with marketing progress. You may well look poorly prepared if you are unable to answer basic questions about current initiatives.

Find original content

People often groan to themselves when someone tells them a joke that they've heard before. They fix a grin on their face, fake a laugh and think to themselves, 'That joke is as old as it is told' or, worse still, 'The same schmuck told me the same joke two days ago'.

New ideas and information excite and challenge people. Old ideas and information, when dressed up as new, can also excite people. However, old ideas and information have little impact when they are repeated in their original form, except to historians.

When we watch the news on television, we often become bored because it resembles the news we heard the night before: war in (insert country name); car crash kills (insert number); sex scandal involving (insert name of politician, member of royal family or Hollywood star); human interest story about (insert species of animal). The formula for the news is old and tired. We only become excited when there is some new and sudden crisis. It interests us because it is new.

When preparing for communication, it is worth keeping this phenomenon in mind. The audience will be more interested if you present original content than if you recycle old jokes and old ideas. For instance, we all know about the greenhouse effect. If you are giving a presentation on the environment, you are better off doing some research and finding new examples of the detrimental effects of greenhouse gases than repeating the environmentalist mantra, 'The greenhouse effect is bad, we are all going to die'. This may be true but, sadly, it is no longer interesting. The same information can be presented with more impact if you prepare new and interesting examples.

Another situation in which this principle applies is job interviews. Employers often interview many people for one position. The person they employ is usually the one who stands out in some way. If you present your skills in a new and interesting fashion during the interview you are more likely to distinguish yourself from the other candidates. For instance, if the interviewer asks you to recall a stressful moment when you had to think quickly, talking about the time you helped fight bushfires is far more interesting than the time you were playing basketball and needed two points to win with thirty seconds on the clock. While you should not make up anecdotes, you should think laterally and find original examples from your own life experience.

HARNESS NERVOUS ENERGY

Nervousness is a major impediment to effective communication. Almost everyone admits that they become nervous when they have to speak to a large audience. Nerves can be crippling for any speaker. An attack of nerves can have numerous symptoms: time slows down, hands become clammy, the brow dampens with perspiration, the voice quavers, the mind goes blank, the eyes have difficulty focusing, the stomach tightens, the mouth dries, and dizziness takes over.

It is no surprise that we become nervous when we have to speak in public. When we speak to an audience, we know that we are being assessed. Whether we are talking to a group of people at a social gathering or making a speech at a wedding, the same question passes through our minds: will these people accept me? Fear of not being accepted lies at the core of our nervousness about speaking in public. In fact, numerous surveys have found that public speaking is our number one fear, ahead of death, which is number two. As comedian Jerry Seinfeld said, 'That means that at a funeral, most people would prefer to be in the casket than giving the eulogy'.

Some people try to ease their nervousness by asking themselves a rhetorical question: what is the worst thing that can happen to me? They assume that the answer is 'nothing much'. However, the consequences of performing badly are often significant — rejection or non-acceptance. This is why most of us are nervous before job interviews, meetings with teachers, major speeches and important meetings, because the worst thing that can happen is that we will not achieve the objectives we have set for ourselves.

Nervousness is a vicious circle. We get nervous because we are worried that we won't perform well. This, in turn, reduces the effectiveness of our performance, which means we are even more nervous next time we have to speak. With commitment, however, anyone can overcome nervousness.

There are three steps to conquering nerves by harnessing nervous energy:
1. Understand that nerves stem from a lack of confidence in your ability
2. Think positively
3. Channel your natural performance energy.

Understand that nerves stem from a lack of confidence

Many people are nervous about speaking in public because they don't believe they know how to do it well. Although most of us know how to speak, very few people are fortunate enough to have been taught how to speak effectively, and for these people communication becomes a 'hit and miss' affair.

Those who regularly deliver speeches in public develop their own techniques to overcome their fears, but for the vast majority of people, speaking in front of even a small audience brings about the same sick feeling as being pulled over by the police. As you become more confident in your ability, your nervousness will decrease.

Positive thinking

We have already mentioned that fear of acceptance is the primary cause of nervousness. To overcome this fear, it is often helpful to visualise your success before you speak. Try to see what you hope to achieve. This doesn't mean that you should be overconfident; rather, you should seek to reassure yourself that success *is* possible.

Performance energy

The nervous energy most people feel before speaking in front of an audience is the first phase of the 'adrenalin rush'. By the time they stand up to speak, they are almost shaking with fear. This 'rush' can be harnessed in several ways, and can substantially improve your performance.

• **Control your voice and breathing.** A quavering voice is one of the key signs of nervousness. Similarly, some speakers lose their breath, and have to gasp for air at inappropriate moments during their speech. Fortunately, both these problems are easily overcome.

The best way to prevent voice problems is to practise reading aloud. You could read bedtime stories to your children or read aloud to yourself. This will help you learn to breathe properly while speaking.

Another technique is to focus on your breathing immediately before your speech. The advice 'Take three deep breaths' is particularly useful in this context. Make sure you continue to breathe evenly throughout your presentation or speech. If at some point you pause for dramatic effect, use it to your advantage and take a deep breath.

You can prevent your voice quavering by varying the volume of your speech. Similarly, if you make an effort to enunciate your words, your voice will quaver less and you will not sound as though you are rushing through your speech.

- **Use your hands.** When people are nervous, often their hands shake. Effective hand gestures are an easy way to harness nervous energy. If you use strong, positive gestures, your hands will not betray your nervousness to the audience.

Try not to hold onto unnecessary objects such as pens or spectacles — they will detract from your speech and greatly diminish you ability to use confident and appropriate hand gestures. (See Chapter Four.)

It is advisable to stand still while you are speaking. Much nervous energy, which could be invested in hand gestures, is wasted if you wander around or shift your weight from one leg to the other while speaking. Excess movement will also distract the audience.

PLAN THE MEDIUM

In most instances of communication the medium is predetermined. In some situations, however, you will be able to choose the medium. If this is the case, you need to consider how formal you want to be, how large you want the audience to be, whether you want to be asked questions, and so on. When making decisions like this, it's important to consider what medium will best enable you to achieve your objectives. It is essential to realise that you must assess and plan *how* you will present your message as well as focusing on the content of the message. You should bear in mind the following two points:

1. When planning communication, a tactical assessment of the most suitable medium for that communication must be made.
2. Having chosen the medium, it is just as important to plan the style of communication as it is to plan the content of the communication.

In 1988, Roger Ailes, an international communications expert, coined the catchphrase, 'You are the message'. As we shall see in Chapter Four, everyone can improve the way in which they speak. Before addressing the specifics of speaking styles, however, it is necessary to understand that the impact of any communication is not only determined by what is said, but also by the way in which it is said.

It's all in the spin

Sometimes it is preferable to let people first hear the facts without commentary before later presenting them with an analysis and a potential solution. This enables the audience to focus on the relevant issues at the outset.

For instance, the 'you're up the creek without a paddle approach', is often very effective in focusing people's minds on the issues facing them and the task ahead. In this case you lay before the audience a series of facts which, when taken together, are evidence of a dire state of affairs. Once the seriousness of the situation has sunk in, the audience will be much more engaged and willing to listen to your analysis and commentary.

Another approach is the 'pot of gold at the end of the rainbow'. Essentially you use the same facts as in the 'up the creek' approach, but put a different 'spin' on it. Instead of emphasising the negative, you talk about the great possibilities that are available and the huge potential that exists. Once the audience is excited about the prospects you have laid out, you can bring in the twist — the huge effort that will be required to get there.

In deciding what spin to put on a set of facts, think about how you expect the audience to react. If they tend to be somewhat apathetic and difficult to engage, the 'up the creek' approach may be a good way to jolt them out of their indifference. On the other hand, it can be fairly confrontational, so you need to remember that people tend to blame the person who delivers the bad news.

In both situations you will be presenting similar information, but in a different style. You must choose the spin which presents the information in the form best tailored to your desired objective.

The spin you place on a particular story can make all the difference between acceptance and rejection. Part of the reason for this is that many people have a tendency to hear what they want to hear and believe what they want to believe. For instance, if you say to an employee, 'You've done a really terrific job here. We're all really impressed. Most importantly, you've shown us that we can really trust you. Now, we have a very important job that we need you to do in a salt mine in Siberia. It's not glamorous, but it's very confidential and you're the only person we really have enough faith in', he may actually believe you. He may convince himself that what looks like a punishment is actually a reward because, after all, that is what he wants to believe.

The style of presentation

The style of presentation you adopt should always be a conscious choice. As we discussed in Chapter One, the tone you adopt should be determined by the objectives of the communication rather than by your emotions. You cannot know what style of presentation will be appropriate until you have analysed your objectives.

You may have to disguise your enthusiasm for a particular course of action because you are trying to appear objective and neutral about a number of options. Conversely, sometimes it may be necessary to emphasise your enthusiasm in order to convey a strong and positive impression. Either way, the style should be consciously chosen rather than determined by your mood.

It is crucial to understand that different styles of presentation produce different responses from an audience. This has nothing to do with the words spoken; rather it is the response that is created by a certain tone of voice, style of hand gesture, or volume or speed of speech. Just as you choose your words carefully to produce a response from the audience, so must you choose an appropriate style of presentation.

Before we examine specific tools and devices that can be used to generate different emotions in an audience (see Chapter Four), it is necessary to understand the various forms that communication can take. It is crucial to consider this before speaking so that you can determine the best approach.

Proactive, reactive or interactive communication

Oral communication can be divided into three broad categories: proactive, reactive or interactive.

Proactive communication is initiated and controlled by the speaker. Speeches and presentations are good examples of proactive communication. In this setting the communicators have the power: they decide what material to present and how it will be presented.

Reactive communication is a response to an invitation to communicate. The best example of reactive communication is a job interview. In that forum, the subject matter and direction of the discussion are determined by the interviewer. The interviewee is responding, usually in a calculated fashion, to the interviewer. The interviewer has the power and the control over the situation.

Interactive communication is somewhere between proactive and reactive communication. An example of this is a meeting in which information is presented and sought by both parties. In this instance, the control of the communication is more evenly distributed than it is in proactive or reactive communication.

Whether a communication is proactive, reactive or interactive will influence the style that you adopt when speaking. In some job interviews, for example, it will be apparent that the employer is seeking a confident, motivated and powerful individual. If so, it will be necessary for the applicant to take greater control of the interview. She will need to redress the power imbalance of the reactive communication to show the interviewer that she is a strong individual.

In other interviews this approach would be completely inappropriate. The employer might be looking for someone who can take orders and who will not 'rock the boat'. In this case, attempting to reverse the power balance of the interview will threaten the employer and the candidate will be unsuccessful.

In each of these situations, it is essential that you have determined beforehand the style of communication that will best help you achieve your objectives.

Sometimes when you are giving a speech, an essentially proactive communication, you will want the audience to feel more involved and included. This can be achieved by adopting a more interactive style, for instance by asking members of the audience for questions or examples. Similarly, certain words can have an inclusive effect on audience members. If you use the term 'we' throughout your speech you will create the impression that you and the audience are 'in this together'. If the objective of the communication is to create a sense of camaraderie or unity, then this is a good tool to use.

KEY POINTS

Know your audience
- The more you know about the audience, the more effective your communication will be
- Pitch your message at the audience's needs and wants, not at your level of interest
- Know what the audience responds to and tailor you message accordingly

Be an expert
- You must be an authority on your subject

Be original
- Original material can make common ideas interesting and engaging to the audience

Harness nervous energy
- It is important to use nervous energy to your advantage

Choose the right spin
- You can get the same message across with a carrot or a stick; you need to look at your audience to work out which will be more effective

CHAPTER THREE

CREATE AN EFFECTIVE STRUCTURE

Time is God's way of keeping things from happening all at once
ANONYMOUS TEXAN GRAFFITI

The importance of preparing the content of your communication, as discussed in Chapter Two, is clear. How can you communicate effectively if you don't know what you want to say? What many people don't realise is that great content is not enough. You may well have all your facts, figures and arguments prepared, but the structure in which you present this material is just as important as the substance, and will be crucial to the effectiveness of the communication.

Without an appropriate structure, a speech, a presentation, or even a conversation, is just a collection of random thoughts. Your thoughts may be brilliant, but without an appropriate structure to tie them together, they will be unintelligible. A clear, coherent structure makes all the difference between a communication that would prompt the comment, 'Well, there were some good ideas there, but . . .', and one that is effective and gets the message across.

When reading this chapter, at first you might think that taking such a structured approach will look too formal and contrived. When you speak, however, a well-defined structure will simply make the material easier to follow.

Creating a good structure is like preparing the canvas before you paint your masterpiece.

PART A: KEEP IT CLEAR AND SIMPLE

PREPARE THE STRUCTURE

Keep it simple

The slogan of US President Bill Clinton's election team in 1992 was 'KISS — Keep it Simple, Stupid' (not 'Keep it Stupid, Simple', as Bush's campaign team sometimes claimed).

KISS worked for President Clinton and it can work for you.

The most common mistake made in oral communication is the failure to keep the message simple. Many people forget how difficult it is to take in material aurally. In a twenty-page paper it is possible to cram in an enormous amount of detail; footnotes, for instance, can hold a wealth of detailed material. In a twenty-minute speech, however, most of that detail is wasted and will only detract from the effectiveness of the presentation.

In written communication, the more concise and clear you can be the better. However, if you are a little long-winded and your argument is somewhat more complex and detailed than it needs to be, it's no great tragedy; it just means a little more work for the reader. It is also quite easy for the reader to skip those details in which they have little interest.

In oral communication the story is quite different. If the audience does not comprehend a particular point the first time, they can't flip back a page and read it again. If the information is too detailed, they will simply 'tune out'. That is why it is so important to keep your message clear and simple. Keeping your message *simple*, however, doesn't mean that your communication must be *simplistic*. The difficulty in mastering this art lies in maintaining the depth and complexity of your message while delivering it in a clear and simple manner.

The importance of keeping your delivery simple can be seen from the complexity matrix on page 54. This matrix is a useful tool for analysing your speaking style or a particular presentation. It demonstrates that you should strive for communication that is simply and concisely presented, but rich in substance and insights.

In Quadrant I, the communication is concise and clear without being overly simplistic. A significant and substantial message is effectively communicated. If you can remain in Quadrant I, you will present a useful message in a 'user-friendly' manner. To reach this quadrant, however, you need to be able to distil and synthesise complex material into easy-to-follow bullet points (see pages 56 and 73).

In Quadrant II, the communication is simple but shallow. In this case, the audience tends to think, 'Why did we bother turning up?'. While the material may be easy to follow, it is also simplistic, something which the audience is likely to find pointless and patronising. Remember that you need to take substantive material and present it concisely; don't just take a shortcut by choosing simplistic and shallow material to start with.

Quadrant III is typical of speakers who are more used to written than oral presentations. Their approach tends to be, 'Well, I've written a brilliant 100,000 word doctoral thesis, so I'm jolly well going to read it out and really impress this audience'. Certainly, some members of the audience will be impressed, but generally they will not be interested and involved, and the communication will not be effective. There is no point in presenting great material if you cannot put it in a form that the audience can understand and be captivated by.

Exhibit 3.1 *Complexity matrix*

Presentation	*Simple*	**I** – Concise – Interesting – Easy to follow	**II** – Shallow – Unmemorable
	Complex	**III** – Detailed but tedious – Alienates the audience	**IV** – Difficult to follow – Speaker out of depth
		Rich/depth	*Simplistic/ shallow*

Substance of speech

Quadrant IV communications are the most difficult to listen to. These speakers are substantially out of their depth and are trying to disguise their blinding glimpses of the obvious as deep and sophisticated insights. Some members of the audience will be fooled, but most will simply be appalled. This approach is somewhat similar to that of a speaker who uses long and complex words to impress the audience — it just doesn't work.

The three-point presentation

The three-point presentation is one of the keys to effective communication. It enables the audience to follow exactly what you are saying, and is invaluable in presenting your message in a clear and concise manner.

Suppose you have written a thesis in which you outline and analyse the thirty-seven arguments that justify

President Truman's decision to drop a nuclear bomb on Hiroshima. You have then been asked to give a presentation on the subject. In a twenty-minute presentation you cannot go through all these reasons, nor do you need to.

It is far more effective to present only three reasons why Truman was right. For example, 'Truman was right to drop the bomb. Some have criticised his decision, but there are three principal reasons why I believe he made the right choice. First, it brought about a rapid end to the war with Japan. This prevented further lives being lost through prolonged war . . . Second . . . Third . . .'. Then discuss each reason in detail. You can allude to other factors, but it is unnecessary to talk about them in depth. Finally, in your summary you can remind the audience of the three reasons. This doesn't mean that you have ignored thirty-four of your thirty-seven points; rather, you have summarised the principal issues into three main issues.

Because you have presented your material clearly, the audience will understand what you've said and will feel involved. Your talk may even lead to a constructive debate. Someone will be able to say, 'Well, I accept your first two reasons, but disagree with your third because . . . Moreover, these reasons are outweighed by the damage that was done to the world's geopolitical stability'.

Some people believe that their presentation is too sophisticated and their material too detailed to be summed up adequately in three points. They are wrong. Any oral presentation can be conveyed in three clear, simple points. You may choose to distribute a more detailed paper as well, but it is a mistake to attempt to read that paper out.

Of course, the notion of using only three points need not be a hard and fast rule. Some presentations may be better suited to two points or four points. But when you find you're starting to reach double figures, it's time to go back to the drawing board and start cutting your material back to a reasonable number of points.

How to sort your material into three points

Before you can put together a clear, three-point presentation, you need to lay out all the material for your consideration, as you would empty out all the pieces of a jigsaw puzzle before you started to assemble it.

Once you have determined your objective (Chapter One) and done the background preparation (Chapter Two), you should list all the points and examples you think you might want to use. A brainstorming session can be useful for this purpose.

Once you have made a long list, critically analyse each point. You need to determine how relevant each point is to your communication. Some will be essential, others will merely be interesting. Begin by noting the crucial points without which you have no case. Focus on putting together the skeleton material, the material that conveys the bare minimum necessary to make your case. Later you can embellish your presentation with interesting but less relevant material, if appropriate. This may be unwise, though, as it could distract the audience from the focus of your presentation.

The next step is to group the main points into categories. Your aim is to reduce your jumbled list into general themes. For instance, if you are preparing a presentation that explains why you support the death penalty, you might put together a long list of possible points. You would then sort these into three main categories:

1. The death penalty is a deterrent against crime
2. The death penalty is an effective means of punishment for the most evil criminals
3. The death penalty removes evil from society.

Once you have sorted your points, you will be able to prepare a clear presentation based around these three issues. There are other issues that you could include — criminals cannot escape from gaol if they have been executed, taxpayers do not have to bear the cost of feeding and housing criminals — but they're not necessary. It is generally counter-productive to risk diluting the impact of your central points by raising peripheral issues.

Brevity is a mark of clarity

'I have written you a long letter because I did not have time to write you a short one.' This quote neatly summarises the skill and time it takes to be succinct. Fortunately it is a skill that can be learnt, and one that can only enhance the effectiveness of your communication. Just as the objective of a game of golf is to play as few shots as possible, so the basic objective of effective communication is to make your point as well as possible in as few words as possible (although we make some allowances for elegance of speech and humour).

In any oral communication, time is always limited. In some cases there will be an explicit time limit, after which the chairperson will start giving you wind-up signals; in other cases, your time will be limited by your audience's attention span. In either situation, the more brief and concise your delivery, the greater your impact will be.

Anyone can make their point given an hour or two to drone endlessly. What shows real skill is the ability to distil complex and detailed subject matter into a concise and clear ten-minute presentation. Never feel that the longer you speak, the more you will be able to say; you will be able to communicate more, with greater impact and clarity, by saying less.

Don't overestimate your audience's attention span

No matter how enthralling a presentation is, many people find it difficult to concentrate for long periods of time. The more detailed your presentation, the more difficult it will be to sustain the audience's attention. If you can present your material in fifteen minutes rather than twenty-five, you will find that it is much easier to maintain the audience's interest.

Prepare a strong opening and closing

Many speakers find that they are quite comfortable speaking with only an outline to guide them. This outline briefly lists the main points, but does not contain any substance or detail about *how* to convey those points. This approach can be very effective if you are confident and can fill in the gaps. However, even if you are able to master this technique successfully, it is generally a mistake to make spontaneous opening or closing remarks.

A strong opening

Your opening remarks are your opportunity to seize the audience's attention. If you open badly, the rest of your speech can be doomed. If the audience is not enthralled by your opening remarks they may switch off, and your remaining comments will be like pearls cast before swine.

Many speakers have blown their whole presentation because of inappropriate opening comments. A doctor turned politician speaking at a fundraising dinner began his speech with a rather crude joke about a well-known actor and a prostitute. He then followed up with a joke about a man suffering from impotence. He raised barely a titter from the thousand-strong audience, and quite a large number of people walked out. His opening remarks almost destroyed a promising political career.

Plainly, it is important to open well. A strong opening will have different characteristics depending on the circumstances. If you are making an after dinner speech at a school reunion and you don't start with an extraordinarily amusing anecdote about your school days, then the going might soon become tough. However, if you are presenting a sales report to a board meeting, a couple of opening jokes might well prove fatal. In this case, a strong, confident introduction to your material and a quick summary of the major points is most effective.

Never start by talking about how difficult it was trying to find something to say, how funny your speech is going to be, or how you hope you don't offend anybody. It is only on rare occasions that someone can make comments like this and get away with it. More often than not, it is simply embarrassing for the audience, who has to sit through a talking cliché.

We once attended a dinner in honour of a well-liked chief executive, who happened to be well known as a self-publicist — he would go to great lengths to get his picture in the paper. The keynote speaker began his speech by saying, 'When I heard that Jim had announced that he was *retiring*, I understood that he meant this only in the narrowest sense of the word'. This was an excellent opening — it was witty and introduced the subject of the evening effectively. Another example of an excellent opening is John F. Kennedy's opening comments at a fundraiser. After a warm welcome he said: 'I am deeply touched, but not as touched as you are.'

Many speakers like to start their address with a quote from someone famous or at least witty. However, this is seldom effective. You should generally be wary of beginning or ending a speech with someone else's words. What does it show? That Winston Churchill or John F. Kennedy were very witty and eloquent? So what? The audience will only form a favourable impression of you if they are impressed by *your* words. It won't help you if they are impressed by the person that you quote.

A strong closing

Your closing is as important as your opening. It is your

closing that the audience will remember after you have finished in your presentation (if, indeed, it was memorable). It is your last opportunity to leave them with a favourable impression.

A good closing will leave the audience feeling positive about your material, you personally, and the points that you have made. A weak closing can undo most of your good work. The audience may focus on your poor conclusion and forget the wealth of material that went before.

If all else fails, ending a presentation with a summary of your key points can be reasonably effective. Generally, however, a better closing will deliver some special insight or somehow touch the audience. For instance, in President Nixon's 'Au Revoir' speech (page 170) his closing lines were: '. . . only if you have been in the deepest valley can you ever know how magnificent it is to be on the highest mountain'.

A closing does not have to be as inspiring as Nixon's, however, to be effective. We once attended a dinner party at our local sailing club where the guest speaker finished by saying, 'You know, usually I find these sorts of dinners very tedious — having to sit up the back and listen quietly for half an hour while some pompous stuffed shirt tells self-serving stories — but tonight I've really enjoyed myself, so thank you for inviting me'. This closing was effective because it was witty and self-deprecating.

Prepared spontaneity

Very few people can deliver totally off-the-cuff remarks effectively. Many people, however, *appear* to be able to. The secret is prepared spontaneity. The key to prepared spontaneity is extemporaneous speech.

How to prepare an extemporaneous presentation

In almost every case, the ideal approach to a presentation,

a public speech, or even an important one-to-one discussion, is *extemporaneous*. Speaking extemporaneously is a compromise between a speech that is read word-for-word or learnt off by heart and one that is completely impromptu and unprepared.

The key to extemporaneous speech is to prepare the substance of what you will say but not the exact words you will use. It is the difference between a typed ten-page document and one page of bullet points. Both can convey the same basic message, but whereas the former provides fully spelt-out sentences, the latter provides just the basic idea without the detail.

The principle behind this approach is that you *know* the detail that should come below the bullet point. You don't need to write it out in great detail. Instead, you express it in a natural and clear manner when you come to that point. For instance, if you intend to explain that earnings have been flat for the last month because a rise in revenue was matched by a rise in variable costs, this need not be written out at length in your notes for you to be able to speak about it for a couple of minutes. Simply write:

'• revenue and costs up, so profit flat'.

This will remind you to address the relevant issues.

The other advantage of a bullet point list rather than a word-for-word script is that it allows for much greater flexibility. If someone asks a question and you need to move away from the structure you have prepared, it won't cause you any problems. Once you've answered the question, you can just skip to another bullet point. With a script, this can be very difficult. We have seen numerous speakers search through their detailed notes for the answer to a question and then become totally confused when they try to find their way back to their original point. Never allow your notes to become a crutch or an impediment to clear communication.

PRESENT A TRANSPARENT STRUCTURE — USE SIGNPOSTS

What is signposting?

Signposting is a technique by which you clearly signal the structure of your communication to the audience. At the outset you present the audience with a 'map' of where your communication will take them. Then at each key turn-off you notify the audience and tell them where it will lead. Finally, at the end of your presentation, you give the audience a quick reminder of where they have been.

When using this technique, in essence you are saying: 'Here is my introduction. I have three points, which are X, Y and Z. This is point X. This is point Y. This is point Z. This is my conclusion. I have presented three points, X, Y and Z. . .'.

Signposting is a way of presenting material; it has nothing to do to with the information that you actually present. However, it is not a suitable technique for all types of communication. For instance, when proposing marriage, the romance of the moment will not be enhanced by the sexy opening: 'There are essentially three reasons why I believe we should get married. First, because . . . Second, because . . . and third, because . . .' When a mood of emotion and spontaneity is required, signposting will sound too officious to be appropriate. You will generate the wrong mood, not because of your message, but because of the way in which you deliver your message.

When to signpost

Signposting is a suitable technique when you want to sound organised and knowledgeable. It is effective when presenting a strategic plan to the board, giving an address at the annual meeting of your local club, or presenting an action plan to a committee.

Exhibit 3.2 *When to use signposting*

		Emotional	Logical
Setting	*Business/ formal*	Signposting may detract from the emotional power of the message	Signposting usually effective
	Social/ informal	Signposting inappropriate	Signposting often useful, but there is a risk of appearing stilted and wooden
		Emotional ◄────► *Logical*	
		Tone	

For the vast majority of business and professional situations, the impression of a logical and structured approach will be viewed as an asset. In these situations, signposting is an excellent technique to use. While it may seem surprising, not every instance of communication requires the speaker to create an impression of organisation and logic. Moments of passion, humour, anger, confusion and frustration may well call for completely the opposite mood. Signposting is not appropriate, for instance, when you are trying to inspire a netball team before a big match, delivering a eulogy, or giving the toast at a wedding. It is an approach that tends to stifle any impression of emotion. This, however, can be one of its great advantages. Often when people go to ask for a pay increase they are nervous and/or a little apprehensive. Similarly, when someone is asked to justify poor performance, they have a tendency to become defensive. Signposting is an excellent tool in these types of situations precisely because it conveys the impression of strength and self-control. It helps you disguise emotion and replace it with the impression of cool rationality.

When giving a speech or presentation, untrained speakers often slip from one point to the next with barely a pause for breath. They know where they are going, but those listening do not. The impact of the communication is diminished purely because of the way it is presented. Signposting is one way of overcoming this problem.

Signposting is particularly useful if any members of the audience happen to be taking notes. Because you are reiterating your key points, the audience is able to identify those points worth recording while at the same time keeping up with your presentation.

We have often seen speakers who present interesting material in an articulate manner, but who fail to signpost. When they have finished speaking, the audience is usually quite impressed, and has understood and absorbed much of what was said, but often has difficulty remembering key points and issues. When an objective of the communication is for your key points to be remembered, rather than just to create a mood, then signposting is of assistance.

In contrast, a fairly average communicator who clearly signposts throughout a speech can be highly effective. The audience will leave thinking that they've heard a clear and simple explanation. Later they will be able to remember and repeat the speaker's three key points and the issues involved.

How to signpost

Generally, the simplest way of signposting is as follows:

- In the opening sentences, mention that your hypothesis is that 'dogs are better than cats', and that you will be providing three reasons to support your view: 'First, dogs

are more friendly. Second, you can take a dog for a walk. Third, dogs can scare off intruders.'
- In the body of your speech, you expand on these points: 'First, dogs are more friendly. How many times have you come home to be greeted by an enthusiastic cat? . . . Second, you can take a dog for a walk . . . Third . . .'
- In summary, you should again refer to your signposts: 'I believe that dogs are better than cats, and I have provided three reasons to support my belief . . .'

It looks somewhat laboured in the written form, but in oral communication, signposting substantially improves a presentation. Remember, the time which elapses between each signpost when the speech is delivered ensures that the signposting does not sound as obvious as in print.

Use a segue

Signposting allows you to let the audience know where you are going and where you have come from. However, you should try to do it in a manner that does not seem stilted or laboured. While in the example above we suggest that you refer to your three points as 'First . . . Second . . . Third . . .', that should not indicate that you have three isolated issues to cover.

A presentation should always follow a natural, logical train of thought. You should not randomly jump between three isolated, disconnected points. In order to move smoothly from one point to another, it is important to use a *segue*. This is a means of connecting one thought to the next. For instance, in the previous example you might be explaining how dogs are more friendly than cats: 'Your dog is always happy to see you. Fido will come and meet you at the door, wagging his tail. As well as being friendly, dogs are more companionable. They like being taken for walks, which is their second major advantage over cats. After all, how often have you taken a cat for a walk . . .'

Signposting in reactive communication

Most people are willing to acknowledge the benefits of signposting once it has been explained to them. They are happy to use signposting when giving a prepared speech, for instance, but would never think of using it for reactive communication. Even speakers who use signposting frequently for any proactive presentation forget about it when it comes to reactive communication. Instead, they often revert to rambling in a 'consciousness' style. However, signposting is also an effective tool to use in reactive communication.

Signposting will often be useful when answering questions during a job interview. When you are being interviewed by a prospective employer, much of what the interviewers are assessing is your ability to communicate, even if they don't realise that themselves. The ability to think in an organised and logical fashion is a clear advantage. If you adopt a structured approach when answering a question, most interviewers will be left with the impression that you are analytical and logical.

There are some added benefits to this approach. The first is that it can be used to buy you time. If you start an answer with the statement, 'Well, that is very interesting. There are several factors I would like to address in answering your question, the first of which is . . .', then you have obtained twenty seconds to think of the best answer without appearing to be stalling (although it is, of course, quite reasonable for you to take a few seconds after a question to think of an answer — see Chapter Six). Similarly, while you are presenting the first component of your answer, usually the most obvious point, you can be thinking ahead to the other factors.

The second benefit is that signposting, when you become accustomed to using it, actually helps you to *think* in a more structured way.

PART B: SET OUT YOUR IDEAS

THE USE OF NOTES

Some people like to communicate without a 'net'. They do not use notes. Most people, however, find that, when used well, notes can improve the effectiveness of their communication.

Of course, notes are only appropriate in certain contexts. You cannot reasonably respond to a question at a dinner party or a request from a police officer by saying, 'Hold on, I'll just check my notes'. However, in any type of proactive oral communication, such as a presentation or a speech, notes are very useful. These notes should contain information relevant to all aspects of the communication in question.

Most people need to use notes when speaking. Even when they do not think that notes are an absolute necessity, they tend to feel far more comfortable when they have some notes they can rely on. Notes are a like an insurance policy. You may be able to give your presentation without them, but you are much wiser to have them in case of emergency. In a crisis — if you freeze because of nerves or your mind suddenly becomes blank — notes can come to your rescue.

The use of notes is simply a recognition of the fact that most of us have not developed our memory skills to the point where we feel comfortable speaking for any length of time without some form of assistance. Even those with near-perfect memories cannot be certain that they will not succumb to nerves at some stage during their presentation.

As long as you use your notes correctly, and they are not obtrusive, then there is no reason to discard them. The crucial issue is not whether to use notes or to speak without them, but *how* best to use notes when speaking. Used well, notes are hardly noticed by the audience, they help your presentation run more smoothly and ensure that no vital point is forgotten. Used badly, notes encourage you to read your speech word-for-word, and make the audience wish that they had just been sent the presentation to read for themselves.

Why are notes important?

To use notes effectively, you need to understand why you are using them and how they can affect the style of your presentation.

As a reminder of content

The primary reason to use notes is to remember what to say. However, when preparing for reactive communication, such as an interview or a meeting, many people believe that they have no need for notes. They simply wait for the questions and then answer them as they see fit.

Notes, however can often be useful for reactive communication. If you are attending a job interview, for instance, you should always take with you a copy of all the material that you sent to the company when applying for the position. As a bare minimum, you should take your résumé to each interview. Before any interview, you should plan what information from your application you wish to stress during the interview. In such situations, it is handy to have reminder notes — often the best place to write them is on the résumé itself.

Similarly, many interview questions will be open-ended, such as, 'Can you tell me about an occasion that required you to exercise leadership?' or, 'What do you think is your most significant achievement?'. A copy of your résumé may help you to answer these questions by acting as a prompt. You can also use these questions to stress those aspects of your résumé not already covered during the interview. This device is particularly useful, as it is often easy to predict some of the questions that you will be asked.

When used as a reminder of basic information, notes are also useful during technical presentations. Few people are capable of remembering sequences of numbers or large volumes of technical data. Not only do notes allow you to record a great deal of information, but they also mean you have some free time before your presentation. You don't need to spend your time memorising your material, instead you can focus on other aspects of preparation, such as your opening, the structure and the tone.

The reasons for using notes for proactive communication are similar. Many people believe that because they control the communication they don't need notes. They believe that with meticulous planning and preparation, they can deliver a compelling and fluent presentation without notes. This is wishful thinking.

The flow of any presentation can be interrupted. A smoke alarm might go off, a phone might ring, an audience member might interrupt, a colleague might ask a tricky question. There are any number of ways in which a presentation can be thrown off track. Without notes, it is often difficult to regain your thoughts and continue with the presentation. Alternatively, you may be able to continue but not be able to remember where you were up to.

In all of these situations there is an enormous upside, and little downside, to using notes. The benefits of performing without notes — 'Look, Mum, no hands!' — are hard to see. Anyone who has ever lost their train of thought mid-sentence will know the potential dangers of not using notes. Too many speakers expend unnecessary nervous energy out of vanity. Pretending that you don't need to use notes is as vain and dangerous as driving a car without wearing glasses, 'because they don't look natural'.

As a reminder of structure

Notes do not simply remind you of what to say. They have other important benefits that most people don't consider.

When used properly, notes can remind you of the structure of your speech and the order in which you should make your various points. Speakers who scribble random ideas at different points on their page are not making the best use of their notes. As we have already discussed, the structure of any presentation is crucial if you are to be an effective communicator.

Notes help provide structure in a number of ways. Most importantly, notes will determine the order in which material is presented. Material on page six will be delivered after material on page two. Thus, notes can be used to order a speech.

As we discussed on page 54, the best way to present material will often be in the logically structured 'three point presentation'. The points should be listed down the page in order, and then presented in that order. You should be able to look down at the page, see the next point and speak on that issue. There is no need to look down at your notes again until you have finished with that point.

This approach to using notes maximises eye contact with the audience (see Chapter Four) and also ensures that if you lose your train of thought or are interrupted, it will be fairly easy for you to get back on track.

Stage directions

As we have already discussed, when giving a speech, the style of presentation is at least as significant as the content. Your notes should not only record what you will say and the order in which you will make your points, they should also remind you of the style of presentation to adopt when delivering certain parts of your speech. We call these reminders 'stage directions'.

Many people, for instance, speak far too quickly when making a presentation. This is usually a result of nerves. Without reminders, these people will continue to speak too quickly throughout their presentation. If you are a fast speaker who is attempting to improve your speaking style, there are two alternatives available to you. The first is that you simply make a concerted effort to remember to slow down. This approach is unlikely to succeed. You will either forget or, worse still, you will expend unnecessary energy and concentration on an aspect of your style that could easily be remedied. The second, and far more successful, approach is to write a reminder to '*slow down*' on your notes. When you glance down at your notes you will see this stage direction, and it will remind you not to speak so quickly.

Another common stylistic fault of many speakers is that they forget to pause during their speech. The easiest way to remedy this fault is to write the word '*pause*' on your notes. This reminder note can be included at various appropriate points in your speech. Thus, when planning your speech, you can also plan suitable moments for a dramatic pause.

Stage directions can also be a useful device in situations of reactive communication. Many people have certain forms of body language that betray their nervousness — they play with their hands, tap their fingers or continually cross and uncross their legs. If you are aware of your own nervous gestures, then stage directions can be a great way of overcoming the problem. For instance, if you write a reminder on your résumé that reads, '*stop twitching*' or, '*don't tap your pencil*', then whenever you look down at your notes during an interview you will remember to correct the problem, or avoid it entirely. If you do write stage directions on your résumé, however, you should try to avoid letting your interviewer see your notes; they may get the impression that you have over-rehearsed.

There are two important tricks to remember when it comes to writing stage directions on your notes. The first is always to highlight the stage directions, or write them in a different coloured pen or in italics. This will stop you from becoming confused. The second point is to make sure that you *never* read out your stage directions. This advice may sound as if it falls into the 'don't chew glass' category, but a surprisingly large number of speakers make this mistake. During the 'Irangate' hearings, President Reagan inadvertently read aloud a card prepared by his staff, with words to the following effect: if asked about when you knew about the payments, look confused and say . . . If asked whether you knew in advance, pause, and claim not to remember.

There is no worse way to make an important point than to say, 'I firmly believe that we must do more to help disabled people. Pause and smile'. Reading stage directions aloud is one of the few ways in which a speaker can instantly lose all credibility. It is very hard to regain an audience's respect when you have said the words 'clench fist' at a key point of your presentation.

THE MOST EFFECTIVE FORMAT FOR NOTES

The next issue to examine is what you should write on your notes. The form which notes should take is very much a matter of personal preference.

Type your notes

The principal benefit of having your notes typed on a word processor is that it guarantees you will be able to read them. At some stage in our lives, we have all been unable to read our own handwriting. This becomes more likely when we are nervous and are only able to glance quickly at the page rather than read the text carefully. If you are unable to type your notes, take the time to write them legibly.

The other benefit of typed notes is that you can easily keep a copy of them on your computer. It is then a simple job to revise, modify and recycle your notes for use on a different occasion (preferably with a different audience!).

Use double spacing

When typing notes for a speech, always use ample spacing. It is far better to use more pieces of paper than it is to cram your material onto one page. When you are communicating — whether in a presentation, a meeting or a speech — time seems to slow down. Five minutes can seem like an eternity. The slightest pause while you are trying to decipher which point comes next can seem to last forever. You become self-conscious if you have to look at the page for too long to work out where you are up to. Given that you should only be glancing at your notes for a couple of seconds at a time, it is crucial that you have ample spacing between your points so that they are easy to read.

Use bullet points

The best way to write notes effectively is to use bullet points rather than complete sentences. Write down only the key points and then express them in your own words when you come to speak. In one sense, it is like making a diary entry. If you wanted to remind yourself that your flight to Cairo is on Friday, you wouldn't write: 'I fly to Cairo on Friday. I must remember to collect my ticket, pack my bags and drive to the airport'. The simple reminder 'Cairo' would be just as effective.

For some reason, when it comes to preparing a speech, people lose all faith in their ability to speak coherently. Simple reminders work in everyday life for diary entries, shopping lists, reminder notes, telephone messages and any number of other shorthand scribblings. Yet when it comes to preparing for more formal communication, people lose confidence in their ability to follow summarised notes.

There are some people who even write the words 'Ladies and Gentlemen' at the top of their notes to remind themselves to start their speech with the appropriate introduction. Yet no one would write themselves a reminder note before a party that says, 'Make sure you say hello to people' — it should be instinctive. The more you write on your notes, the more likely you are to read your speech word for word.

Waste a third of each piece of paper

Often you will use sheets of paper for your notes, especially if you are using a lectern. It is best in these situations to type only on the top two-thirds of the page and leave the bottom third blank. This ensures that when you look at your notes you will not have to look too far down. When you stand at a lectern, the bottom of a piece of paper will be almost adjacent to your navel. Speakers who have to look down as far as their navel to read their notes will lose too much eye contact with the audience.

What about cards?

Some people prefer to use cards rather than full sheets of paper. One of the advantages of cards is that they are easy to shuffle and reorder. If you decide to replace one point with another, it's easy — just replace a card. When using cards, however, you must be wary of the tendency to write too much and have too many cards. If you write your speech out on cards and then read it verbatim, it looks just as bad as reading from sheets of paper.

Cards also have a real advantage over sheets of paper when there is no lectern or table on which to rest your notes. In situations like this, having to hold a sheet of paper while speaking is an impediment to effective communication. The sheet of paper becomes a physical barrier between you and the audience.

Holding sheets of paper also severely restricts your use of hand gestures. If you have to hold a sheet of paper in front of you, you don't have a free hand with which to gesture. This will greatly reduce the impact of your speech

Exhibit 3.3 *Best man's speech at a wedding*

- Greeting/Welcome
- Anecdotes about groom
  —How we met
  —Sleeping habits
  —Drinking habits
- How he met her
- Anecdotes about bride
  —history
  —wardrobe
- Something nice about couple
- Best wishes (SINCERE)

(SLOW DOWN)

or presentation (see Chapter Four).

If you do decide to use cards it is important to use the right type. They can range in size from that of a business card to that of a video cassette. Usually the best ones to use are those the size of business cards. They fit neatly in the palm of your hand and in no way restrict your use of hand gestures. For presentations on technical issues, however, these cards may be too small. When large amounts of material must be stored on the cards it is more appropriate to use bigger cards.

It is important to remember that if you intend to hold your notes in your hand rather than rest them on a lectern, the cards should be made of cardboard or thick paper. A flimsy piece of paper tends to be more difficult to use, and the sight of a speaker holding a drooping piece of paper is quite disconcerting for the audience.

Transparencies

If you are using an overhead projector for your presentation, instead of writing notes on cards or paper, write them on the borders of your transparencies. That way you can see your comments on the borders, but all your audience sees are the charts. This can be a very effective way of writing notes if your presentation is closely linked to a number of charts. Simply write down a few key points on each transparency. You should also make a note of the main points of interests and the segue; that is, how you will link one transparency to the next.

The transition from one point to another, and particularly from one chart to another, is a crucial element of any presentation. If the transitions are made well, the presentation will be clear and smooth. If not, it can often appear disjointed and be difficult to follow. It is important that there is a clear theme and logical link behind your material; it should not appear to be just a random collection of points.

KEY POINTS

Keep it simple

- Three points are much easier to understand and digest than a dozen
- Be concise — if you are too long-winded or provide unnecessary detail, the audience will lose interest

Prepare a strong opening and closing

- Your opening is crucial to gaining the audience's attention, and your closing will be what they remember; therefore it is important to prepare both in advance

Present a transparent structure

- Signposting makes it easier for the audience to follow your presentation or speech and take notes

Use notes effectively

- Notes eliminate the need to memorise large chunks of material
- Bullet points help you maintain your prepared structure and remind you of the key points
- Stage directions can help you with your style of presentation

CHAPTER FOUR

PRESENT AN EFFECTIVE STYLE

Why can't somebody give us a list of things that everybody thinks and nobody says, and another list of things that everybody says and nobody thinks
OLIVER WENDALL HOLMES

In the 1960 US presidential campaign, Vice-President Richard M. Nixon and Senator John F. Kennedy participated in the first televised presidential debate. It was exciting television. Fifty million Americans tuned in to see the two Presidential candidates talk about their vision for America.

When the debate was over, opinion was divided about who had triumphed. Surveys of TV audiences found that a slim majority thought Kennedy had won. On the other hand, among people listening to the debate on radio, a substantial majority believed that Nixon had won. A look at the historic footage clearly reveals the reason for this difference: Nixon is perspiring profusely and looks flustered on television. While Nixon's arguments and style of speech were more persuasive than Kennedy's, his physical appearance tipped the balance for those with a visual impression of the spectacle.

For the radio audience, there was no visual impact. Judging the debate simply on the substance of what was said and the manner of speech, Nixon bettered Kennedy.

At a debate more than thirty years later, the grand final of the World Debating Championship in Dublin, the style of presentation was again the differentiating factor. In a rather long and involved debate, what made the two speakers from Glasgow really stand out was not just their melodious Scottish accents, but rather their whole style of delivery. Having started with fairly witty jokes, they went on to give amusing and entertaining speeches. For an audience struggling to remain awake, this came as a welcome change from the rather earnest and serious young men who were their opponents.

It was no surprise that by the end of the debate the audience was strongly backing the Glasgow team, who, of course, won the championship. They were not awarded the victory based on style alone, but their ability to capture the audience's attention was certainly a great advantage.

The manner of presentation is what differentiates the truly memorable speaker from someone who simply 'gets the job done'. For instance, had history seen Sylvester Stallone rather than Martin Luther King deliver the famous 'I have a dream' speech on 28 August, 1963, the moment is unlikely to have been particularly memorable. Exactly the same speech would have produced an enormously different response purely as a consequence of the style of presentation.

Similarly, had President Kennedy delivered his Presidential Inauguration Address on that cold January day in 1961 by post, and told Americans 'to ask not what your country can do for you' in writing rather than in person, the quote may not have found its way into every Dictionary of Quotations. In this instance, it was the moment and delivery of the presentation as well as the identity of the speaker, and not simply the words spoken, that gave the speech its extraordinary impact.

In many ways, *what* a speaker says is not nearly as important as *how* the speaker says it. In 1968, an article entitled 'Communication Without Words' appeared in *Psychology Today*. In that article, Professor Albert Mehrabian

Exhibit 4.1 *Factors influencing effective communication*

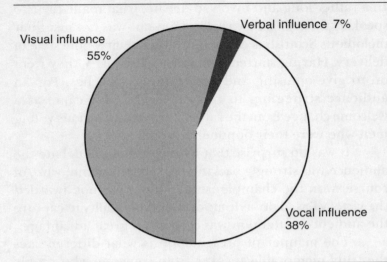

Visual influence 55%

Verbal influence 7%

Vocal influence 38%

argued that up to 93 per cent of a speaker's impact on the listening audience is determined by non-verbal factors. According to his theory, the effectiveness of a speech is influenced by three factors: 7 per cent of the total impact of the speech is a function of what was said (*verbal influence*); 38 per cent of its impact is determined by how it was said (*vocal influence*); and 55 per cent of its impact is determined by the visual impression that the speaker creates (*visual influence*).

Professor Mehrabian's findings are not surprising. Advertising on television is more influential than advertising on radio because of the visual component. When offered the choice, politicians choose to appear on television rather than radio because of the increased impact that the medium offers. The same speech delivered on television and on radio will have a greater effect on the television audience because people can make a visual assessment of the speaker as well as an assessment of what the speaker has said.

Effective communication is as much about form as it is about substance. Some people find communicating in an effective style more difficult to master than others. But getting it right is worth it.

THE STYLE OF SPEECH
The value of an effective speaking style

If you try to recall the speakers who have most impressed you, it will generally be their style of presentation that sticks in your mind. Numerous politicians, for instance, have speech writers, but what makes one more impressive than another is their ability to communicate the message which they are presenting.

Sometimes the style and substance of a speech are difficult to disentangle. Was John F. Kennedy's inaugural address a brilliant set of words by Theodore Sorensen or an inspired performance by JFK? Some would say both, but probably Sorensen deserves more of the credit than Kennedy.

There is no 'ideal' speaking style that you should try to emulate. Generally, you will be most effective when speaking fairly naturally. But if your natural speaking style involves mumbling, speaking very quickly, or gazing down at your feet, then some finetuning may be necessary.

An effective speaking style does not come easily for everyone. Some people are naturally more witty, charming, articulate and fluent than others. However, it is a mistake to believe that you cannot change your style. Everyone can become an interesting and engaging speaker. In this chapter we discuss some simple techniques — tricks of the trade — that can be learnt by anyone.

It is important that you learn these skills for all forms of communication. Too many people adopt the attitude that they will not worry about their speaking style until they are called upon to make a public speech. This is an unwise attitude to adopt, for several obvious reasons:

- *An interesting and convincing style of communication is called upon every day in business and in personal life*. People are always on show and being compared to their colleagues, and the ability to communicate effectively 'fast-tracks' any career. Not all communication in a professional environment is planned. Every time you meet a client or a senior manager, your communication skills are being assessed, either consciously or subconsciously. If a presentation has to be made at short notice, the chronic mumbler will have no time to learn how to be entertaining, articulate or effective.

  The same applies when you see your bank manager about a mortgage or visit your child's school to meet the teachers and the principal. Just as you are judging them in very short period of time, so they are judging you. You don't get much opportunity to see them in action, so you assess them based on the way they communicate. You come away thinking, 'What a nice woman, she seemed very bright and lively' or, 'What a fool. What could my kids possibly learn from him?'. By the same token, your effectiveness as a communicator is the principal basis on which you will be assessed. It is therefore worth doing well.

- *The hesitant speaker, who seems always to get flustered, will not be chosen to make important presentations*. The boring or nervous communicator will not be asked to make presentations to clients or senior management if there is an alternative presenter who already knows how to deliver an interesting presentation. The ineffective communicator will be overlooked for such opportunities. Few people will accept the promise, 'Just give me a chance, boss. I'll learn to be interesting in the time that I have before the speech'.

  This applies to every facet of life. The people whose

views are sought at parent's meetings, at work, or at a meeting of the local bridge association are those who can communicate well. You might have the best ideas in the world about how to transform your local yacht club into a world class institution, but no one will be interested if you are not an effective communicator.

- *Anyone who has time to prepare for their communication should not be spending that time learning the basics of an effective style.* This is commonsense, in the same way that someone should not have to learn the basics of mathematics before attending a high-powered meeting about venture capital. An effective style of communication is a basic skill that most you should have in your repertoire.

  If two people have the same amount of time to prepare a speech but one speaker must also use that time to learn how to present effectively, it's clear which speaker will fare better.

- *The inability to communicate effectively becomes a psychological hurdle to further achievement.* Those who communicate well can throw themselves forward in the workplace and in social activities, and are successful. In contrast, those who cannot communicate in an interesting and entertaining style believe that they have some secret to hide. They become like school students who cannot read. They dread being asked to make presentations, they are fearful of being asked questions in meetings. Rather than seeing such questions as an opportunity to shine and promote their careers, they see it as an opportunity to commit career-limiting moves. This psychological barrier is not just a barrier to communication but a barrier to career success and social interaction.

It is crucial to master an effective speaking style as soon as possible. It is not a skill which anyone can put off acquiring until it's needed — it is a skill that is always necessary.

Be committed to improvement

When trying to persuade people that they must concentrate on improving their speaking style, we have come across two categories of negative response. They are:

1. **Denial** — 'I already know how to speak, I've been doing it all of my life' or, 'I did a bit of public speaking at school as a kid, so I already know how'. People in this category deny that there is any need for them to improve their style of communication. They think that the importance of style is overrated. They prefer to concentrate on the content of the communication and let the style 'take care of itself'.

2. **Futility** — 'I am a naturally boring speaker, that's just the way I was born' or, 'I get so nervous and my hands just seem to get in the way'. These people lack self-confidence. They believe that the ability to communicate effectively is biologically determined. They think that you either have the entertainment gene or you don't. This is an essentially pessimistic and defeatist approach.

Both these types of people must change their outlook if they are to become effective communicators. It is easy to become a more effective communicator. The skills are so easily learnt that immediate improvement is possible for anyone.

As long as you approach the process of improving your skills with the right objectives in mind, you will make great progress. You should be realistic about what you want to achieve. If you are committed and open to self-criticism and constructive comments from others, you too can build an effective style of presentation.

Although your manner of presentation is of fundamental importance, substance is also a crucial aspect of communication (see Chapter Two). Some speakers believe that their natural eloquence and perspicacity will carry them through any occasion. They will breeze into a meeting unprepared and their presentation will lack substance. This chapter will help you develop an effective style; however it is as well to remember that style is not enough — you also need substance.

MANNER OF DELIVERY

Language

Use plain English

The style of language that you use will vary substantially depending on the context of your communication. However, plain English is almost always the most effective. Generally, slang, colloquialisms and informal phrases should be avoided. Jargon should be used sparingly, and only when you're sure that everyone will understand the words you're using and that there isn't a simpler way of saying it.

Using long or complicated words won't impress anyone. People are far more impressed by a speaker who can make a point using simple, clear language. Dealing with lawyers used to be a nightmare because of their notorious inability to give a straight answer or to prepare a document that anyone without a law degree could understand. Pages were full of 'heretofore' and 'whereas the party of the second part'. But now that there has been a movement towards plain English in the law, lawyers are learning to speak clearly, and to draft documents that may be readily understood. This trend is part of a wider movement away from oratory and pretension, and towards plain English usage.

Plain English is more effective because it is clearer and easier for the audience to understand. There is simply no point in using a panoply of multisyllabic and quin-tessentially pretentious words to make a point when simple, everyday words will do the job more effectively.

No one will be impressed if you use complicated phrases and long words. People will simply be disappointed by your failure to express yourself clearly.

Short sentences

The key to effective plain English is to use short sentences. You do not need to use long, rambling sentences that try to say everything in one go, but end up confusing the audience because they cannot remember where the sentence started and what its original purpose was, particularly in respect of complex issues that require a number of propositions to be layered upon each other to establish the eventual point that may, in itself, be far from obvious, at any particular moment in time or in respect of any issue that may develop or need some degree of clarification or explanation at the time or at some later point (depending upon the context of the communication (given that some communications will occur in different circumstances to others) or the audience present).

Short sentences work better. They are clear. The audience can follow what you're saying, one proposition at a time. For instance, if you are trying to prove that Fido has fur: 'Fido is a dog. All dogs have fur. Therefore Fido has fur'. You could easily have said it in one sentence, but why bother?

Short sentences have another advantage. They are punchy. They make your speech more interesting. They make it seem pacy. If you are naturally boring, you will seem more interesting.

Choose your words carefully

Some people have a tendency to use words that subliminally detract from their credibility. 'I honestly believe that . . . ' or, 'I'm not exactly sure of this but . . . ' or, 'I think that I once read. . . '. You need to be conscious of the message this type of language conveys.

Always project an air of confidence through your choice of words. Don't apologise or justify yourself. If you tell the audience that you 'honestly believe that . . . ' they will wonder if you're telling the truth the rest of the time.

Try to avoid casting doubts on your own arguments. For instance, rather than saying, 'Apparently there are more sheep than people in New Zealand', why not just say, 'In New Zealand, there are more sheep than people'. The 'apparently' is only there because you have not actually gone out and counted heads yourself. So what? No one expects you to. If you are confident enough about the information to repeat it in public, then you should be confident enough to state it as a fact.

Swearing should almost always be avoided. In some contexts you might get away with it, but why take the chance? There is always a risk that you will offend someone or cause them to think less of you. Remember, there are far more effective ways to emphasise a point or get a laugh than by the use of swear words.

Clarity of expression

To become an effective communicator you must always strive for clarity of expression. Some people are tempted to use sophisticated words and complicated grammatical constructions to impress the audience with their eloquence. However, the speaker who can communicate clearly and simply is generally regarded as far more impressive.

Anyone can summarise a newspaper article given ten minutes to do so. But it takes far more thought to be able to summarise the article effectively in two sentences. The art is in being able to read, understand and analyse the article, then articulate its key points in a few short sentences.

People also have a tendency to speak in long, and often incomplete, sentences. This should be avoided. Keep your delivery clear and simple by using short, complete sentences.

Enunciation

Speakers who are difficult to understand are very seldom effective communicators; people simply cannot be bothered to make a great effort to understand them. If you aren't easy to understand the audience will just switch off and nod and smile inanely while you speak.

In everyday speech, we tend to become somewhat relaxed about the way in which we speak. The result is that many words are not pronounced clearly. The audience should not have to struggle to understand every word or guess at words that they don't hear clearly.

When speaking to a group of people, it is of fundamental importance to enunciate each word. You should pronounce each word so clearly that if you were having a normal conversation, it might sound a little forced.

There is a by-product of enunciating each word clearly: if you have limited time and are trying to speak quickly, then the more clearly you enunciate, the better your chances of being understood.

Volume of presentation

Many a speech has failed to hit its mark because the presentation was too loud or too soft.

Basically, the volume of your presentation should be appropriate to the physical surroundings. You should never have to shout; if a room is so big that you'd have to shout to be heard at the back then you should try to arrange some form of amplification, such as a microphone. The only thing worse than sitting up the back and not being able to hear the speaker is sitting up the front and being overwhelmed by someone speaking too loudly.

The best way to ensure that your volume is appropriate is to test the room beforehand. Ask a couple of friends or colleagues to stand at the front and back of the room while you speak from the podium. By trial and error you should be able to identify a level of volume that is comfortable for people in both sections of the room.

If this is not possible, you can prearrange for someone in the audience to signal to you during your presentation. This person should be able to indicate to you whether you are speaking too loudly or too quietly. Another method is to 'read' the audience for signs that your volume is inappropriate. For instance, if people sitting at the back are cupping a hand to an ear or moving forward in their seat, it could be a sign that you are speaking too quietly.

Volume should be varied throughout a presentation to improve the impact. While speakers are often prepared to speak more loudly to emphasis a point, they are often unwilling to speak quietly. Sometimes speaking quietly can be an effective way of emphasising a point. If the audience has to lean forward to listen to you, it may enhance your impact.

Use an appropriate tone

The tone of any presentation is the mood and feel it conveys to the audience. Some situations call for a warm tone, others for a sad or mysterious tone. The appropriate mood can be created by adopting certain expressions, gestures and phrases.

The tone in which you deliver your presentation is crucial to its success. It must be appropriate to the material you are delivering and correspond with the sentiment that you are trying to inspire in your audience. This relates back to your objective, because to adopt the appropriate tone, you need to know what effect you want to have on the audience: do you want to scare them, inspire sympathy, get them 'on side', comfort them, or win them over? It is therefore crucial that you work out your approach before communicating.

The tone you use can also have dramatic impact on the way your message is received. For instance, if you want to deliver the message that the sales force has to start selling greater quantities of high-margin merchandise if the company is ever going to make a profit, you could take a number of approaches.

You could say, in a disparaging tone, 'I'm absolutely fed up. All you do is breeze around all day selling widgets, on which we lose money, but none of you ever bother to try to sell gizmos, which make us money. If things don't improve, heads will roll'.

The alternative is to take a more constructive approach by using a positive and upbeat tone to deliver the same message: 'You have all done well in selling large quantities of widgets over the last quarter — very impressive results. Now that we have built a customer base, over the next quarter we need a much stronger focus on selling gizmos — on which we make a better margin. As you are all aware, the company has been losing money for some time; I firmly believe that we *can* survive and prosper by selling more gizmos in the future'.

While no particular tone is to be encouraged above others, to be effective you must be sure to vary your tone during a presentation. This is commonly referred to as 'light and shade': at some points you will want to be very serious and earnest, but at others you should try to appear more relaxed, perhaps even a little jovial. This is vital if you want to maintain the audience's interest.

Many speakers are monotonous. They fail to vary their tone and pace throughout their speech. One way to ensure that you remember to vary your tone is to include references to tone in your notes (see Chapter Three). Make a conscious effort to vary your tone as you move from one point to another. Use one tone when you are being thoughtfully analytical and another when you are presenting facts. Often, for instance, you will be fairly loud and aggressive when criticising another point of view, but far more melodious and quiet when presenting your own, more reasonable, argument.

Speed of delivery

Avoid speaking too quickly

In casual conversation we often do not notice how quickly we speak. We become used to individual styles of speech quite readily, so there is usually no difficulty in understanding friends who speak very quickly or who mumble. However, in a speech or presentation to a group of people, often not everyone present will be familiar with your particular idiosyncrasies, and may have difficulty understanding you if you 'race' or mumble.

People who have a natural tendency to speak quickly often have a great deal of difficulty slowing down, particularly because they often refuse to believe that they speak so rapidly. One very successful speaker used to write the words *slow down* on every second card that he used in order to remind himself to do just that. (See Chapter Three).

Even speakers who don't normally speak too quickly sometimes 'race' when they are left with less time than they had anticipated; either they are only half way through their material and they suddenly realise that there are only two minutes remaining, or the program is running late, and so their twenty minutes becomes twelve. In either case, the best way to deal with the problem is not to speak more quickly, but to hit only the high points of your material.

If you find that you only have half as long to give your presentation as you had prepared for, then you should make sure that you still have an introduction, body and conclusion, just make them all a little briefer. Avoid some of the more in-depth explanations and allude to them briefly instead, and perhaps leave out some of the less significant points. You should always try to make the best of the time available. It is far better to give a truncated presentation in the time available, than to get only half way through and then have to stop.

The pause

One element of slowing down your presentation is the effective use of the pause. Too many speakers fail to take pauses because they are rushing to get through all their material in the allotted time.

Some speakers, especially those who feel they have a lot to say, tend to speak non-stop for the allotted time, hardly even stopping to take a breath. While you cannot afford to waste the time allotted for your presentation, a pause can be a very effective way to add emphasis to a point and give the audience a short moment to think about what you have said. The pause also helps you vary the pace of your speech and move from one point to another.

In fact, when you are severely rushed for time during a presentation, a pause can often save time. This may sound like a contradiction in terms, but it's true. For instance, you could say, 'The most crucial point that I can make to you is this: [PAUSE] . . . .' The pause may take two seconds but it emphasises what you are about to say. It also takes less time than emphasising the material by saying it quickly and repeating it. There are only a few techniques that can be used to emphasise important material, and the pause is, ironically, one of the least time-consuming.

The pause can also be useful for speakers who use certain terms as a verbal crutch. Those who repeatedly use 'um', 'like', 'you know' or 'Ladies and Gentlemen' can wean themselves off such phrases simply by pausing instead. Verbal crutches are best avoided because they can make you appear nervous or unsure of your material.

Use and misuse of humour

When to use humour

Humour can be a very effective tool for maintaining the audience's attention — it allows you to entertain while informing and persuading. It can help you to reduce tension, make tough news more palatable and deflect criticism.

Humour is not, however, a prerequisite for successful communication. Few of the great speeches in history start with a joke. For instance, President John F. Kennedy's memorable inaugural address in 1961 did not start with 'A funny thing happened to me on the way to the White House . . .'.

Humour is useful in social settings — weddings, birthdays, celebrations — because it entertains people and helps them relax. It can be useful as an ice-breaker in tense situations, or when people don't know each other. Of course, when using humour you should always be mindful of using it appropriately. Humour is a device that, if used prudently, can win warmth and support from any audience. However, it can also easily backfire.

As a rule, humour is not necessary and generally not advisable in presentations in a professional environment. The belief that every presentation needs to start with a joke or a funny story is a trap people frequently fall into. The danger of this approach is that it ignores the significance of the opening minutes of any presentation. Most audiences make an initial assessment of a speaker based on the first minute of their presentation. Few audiences ever change that impression. While first impressions may be deceptive, they are usually enduring, so the opening to any speech is crucial. For this reason, starting a presentation in a light-hearted vein may create the wrong impression.

This brings us back once again to the importance of establishing objectives before commencing any communication. It will be rare in a professional environment for one of the prime objectives of communication to be to persuade the audience that you are funny. Being liked by an audience, respected by an audience, interesting to an audience and appearing funny to an audience are hugely different things. Starting a professional presentation with a joke may 'warm up' the audience, but it is unlikely to create the tone you are aiming for in a business environment.

Another possible downside to telling jokes in a professional context is that peers (and worse, superiors) may form the opinion that you are frivolous. A sad but true phenomenon is that of the worker who is seen as the company's jester. The danger of such a characterisation is that there is no known cure. Once a clown, always a clown.

If in doubt, it is best to play it safe and omit humour. It is not worth risking causing offence, embarrassing yourself or even jeopardising your career simply to get a couple of laughs. It would be of little consolation to have a professional epitaph that read, 'He was the brightest man we ever hired, and the funniest man we ever fired'.

In many other circumstances, however, humour is almost essential — for an after dinner speech, or a toast at a wedding, for example. Remember that you need to tailor your approach to the context of the communication. Below we look at the after dinner speech in detail, as an example of how to proceed.

The after dinner speech

After dinner speeches are always a challenge. Generally, the audience is in the mood to be entertained. With any luck they have had a few drinks and will laugh at virtually anything. You must be careful, however, to judge your audience carefully. Many after dinner speakers fall flat by commencing their speech with a rather crude joke which the audience pointedly failed to laugh at.

There are three keys to giving a successful after dinner speech:

1. **Research your audience.** You must understand what their common thread is — for instance, at a legal convention, jokes about the law will go down well. You

must also understand where to draw the line. Obviously, the type of humour you will use in a speech at a buck's night will be quite different from that which you use to address a gathering of nuns.

2. **A speech is not a stand-up comedy routine.** A series of isolated jokes, even if very funny, is unlikely to go down well. As with any speech, you need a theme, three points and a structured approach (although you should be more relaxed about this than you would in a pre-sentation to the Board). Jokes can be used to reinforce points you are making, but they should not *be* the points themselves.

Humour is a delicate art. While one person may deliver a funny line to howls of laughter, someone else might use the same joke and not even raise a snicker. Humour needs to be natural, spontaneous and directly relevant if it is to be effective. If a joke is not spontaneous it should at least seem to be relevant or vaguely contextual. Complete *non sequiturs* can appear somewhat bizarre to the audience — it is generally not a good idea to start your speech with an old favourite like 'A horse walks into a bar. The bartender asks 'why the long face?', as funny as it might be.

Even if you do succeed in amusing the audience, you must be wary of getting so carried away with your comic prowess that you entirely forget the point you were making and go off on some obscure tangent.

3. **Keep it brief.** Don't speak for too long. Don't take advantage of the audience's friendly disposition. An after dinner speech should be punchy and entertaining. If you can only put together seven minutes of punchy and entertaining material, don't try to stretch it out for twelve minutes. A good seven-minute speech is far better than a dull twelve-minute soliloquy. After all, the object is to entertain, rather than to put the audience to sleep.

Use of repetition

Repetition is a tool used by many persuasive speakers to achieve optimum impact with the audience. While we all know that repetition is when a person repeats certain words or phrases, or an aspect of their presentation, few of us understand that there are different forms of repetition, all of which achieve different results.

There are four types of repetition that we shall examine: simple repetition, puppeteer's repetition, conceptual repetition and bluff repetition.

Simple repetition

The simplest form of repetition we have imaginatively called 'simple repetition'. This is when a speaker utters the same phrase or word twice or more to reinforce its significance. An example of this is when people yell 'Help! Help! Help!'. It conveys the same message as just saying 'help' once, but the words take on a greater impact through their repetition. It is as if the assistance is required three times as urgently purely because of the repetition.

Used in this sense, repetition is a form of *verbal underlining*. The speaker is drawing attention to a more important or significant part of their presentation by repeating it, thus giving the idea greater 'air time'.

To achieve a positive result, you must consider wisely which aspect of your speech is truly worthy of repetition. Often people butcher this technique by repeating inconsequential points. Similarly, some speakers overuse common catch phrases such as, 'Ladies and Gentlemen' or, 'I guess what I'm trying to say is . . .'. This is a mistake and a misuse of repetition. If you remember that the purpose of repetition is to give added emphasis to the repeated phrase, then it becomes obvious that repetition of a phrase like 'ladies and gentlemen' is a waste of time and an irritating affectation.

A related trap that people fall into when using simple

repetition is to highlight an insecurity through their repetition of an inappropriate part of their speech. This concept is best exemplified by Shakespeare in *Hamlet* when Gertrude perceptively declares: 'The lady doth protest too much methinks'. When improperly used, repetition can make you sound a little too insistent.

Perhaps the most effective use of simple repetition as a stylistic tool was Winston Churchill's address to the House of Commons on 4 June 1940:

> We shall not flag or fail. We shall fight in France, we shall fight on the seas and oceans, we shall fight with growing confidence and growing strength in the air, we shall defend our island, whatever the cost may be, we shall fight on the beaches, we shall fight on the landing grounds, we shall fight in the fields and in the streets, we shall fight in the hills; we shall never surrender.

The repetition of the words 'we shall fight . . . ', culminating in the phrase 'we shall never surrender' produces a far greater impact than if Churchill had merely stated 'we shall fight in the following places. . . '. Here repetition was used for dramatic purpose. It was a turn of phrase that somehow magnified the level of commitment of the British people to winning the War.

Puppeteer's repetition

The second form of repetition, puppeteer's repetition, is conceptually similar to simple repetition. It is the device whereby a speaker deliberately repeats those parts of their presentation that they know people will be taking written note of. Like a puppeteer, the speaker is manipulating the audience without the audience noticing.

If you know that members of the audience will be taking notes, it is worth making their task easier by using repetition. If the point is a crucial one, it will be worth repeating anyway for added emphasis. When members of the audience are taking notes and the speaker assists them by repeating the key points, they will warm to that speaker. Audience members who are hurriedly writing down key points are often thinking to themselves, 'I wish she would repeat that point so that I could get it down'. These audience members are pleasantly surprised by speakers who answer this unspoken request.

Puppeteer's repetition is a particularly useful technique for technical presentations, where the speaker is trying to impart large quantities of technical information to the audience. The repetition of crucial formulas or figures is greatly appreciated by members of the frantically scribbling audience. In these situations, the audience may be even more satisfied if the speaker has some copies of the crucial information to distribute to them. If this is not possible, repetition is the next best thing.

Conceptual repetition

The third form of repetition can be described as conceptual repetition. This is a device for reinforcing key points. The speaker makes the same point a number of times but uses different words each time in order to better explain the point. The most obvious example of this form of repetition occurs when a speaker says, 'Maybe if I put that another way then it will become clearer to you'.

Conceptual repetition is often used by politicians during interviews when they have one key point that they want the audience to take away from the interview and so repeat the point in a variety of ways to reinforce it. This technique is particularly useful when dealing with audiences who have little understanding of the information that the speaker is trying to get across. It is a tool commonly adopted by teachers when trying to impart knowledge to their young students.

Conceptual repetition relies, in part, upon an understanding that different people comprehend material in different ways. An explanation that works for some members of the audience may not work for others. Using a couple of different explanations for the same points greatly increases the level of understanding.

Bluff repetition

The final type of repetition is bluff repetition. As the name suggests, this approach involves bluff and illusion. In its crudest form, bluff repetition is when a speaker says, 'There are five reasons that we should do this: they are A, B, C, D, and A again because it is so important'. There are in fact only four reasons, but the speaker creates the impression that there is more weight to the argument by repeating one of the earlier reasons and making it appear to be a totally separate point.

Bluff repetition is useful whenever you want your argument to appear more substantial. This may be because you have to speak for ten minutes but only have five minutes' worth of material, or because you only have a few compelling points but wish to sound more convincing.

Remember, bluff repetition is purely a device of presentation. You are not coming up with more information or arguments, you are simply presenting the material that you have in such a way as to make less look like more.

VISUAL PRESENTATION

Visuals should never detract from the message

Nothing in your visual presentation should detract from what you are saying. Some speakers have a tendency to wander around while they are speaking, use 'windmill' hand gestures or fidget with their hands or notes. This can distract an audience who would otherwise (we hope) be trying to concentrate on what you are saying.

If you are speaking at a lectern, stand upright and lightly hold the lectern at each side. You can then use either hand for gestures. Try to avoid gripping the lectern too tightly: this makes you look as though you are very nervous and are holding the lectern for support.

A common trap many speakers fall into is to grasp a 'security blanket' while speaking. The two most common implements are pens and spectacles. During meetings, people usually have pens in front of them to take notes, and so tend to play with their pens while speaking. If you do this, no great calamity will occur, but it can be somewhat distracting for the audience. Try to free your hands for effective use of gestures.

Use appropriate gestures

The use of hand gestures is very much a 'natural' aspect of speaking; some people use certain gestures while speaking and are not even aware of it. Hand gestures can therefore be difficult to change. Gesturing is important, however, so it is worth putting in the effort to get it right.

There are four sure-fire gestures that you should have in your repertoire — the open hands on the crucifix, the test for rain (one- or two-handed), the 'light bulb point' ellipsis ('Mark my words') and the 'fine thread extrusion'. The benefit of these four gestures is that they are all springboard gestures; that is, they lead to further hand movement because they are uncomfortable positions to maintain for any length of time. (See Exhibit 4.2.)

Skilful gesturing can add to any presentation or speech, and poor gesturing can substantially detract from any presentation. It is frustrating for the audience to listen to and watch an otherwise impressive speaker whose right hand continually darts up and down, apparently of its own accord.

Above all, gestures should be unobtrusive. They should be used to emphasise key points and to add some energy and vigour to a presentation. Your hands, however, do not have to be moving constantly.

Eye contact

Eye contact is one of the key tools of effective communication. If you don't look at the person you are speaking to, you will seem rude. If you look at the person you are speaking to but don't look them in the eye, you come across as dishonest, and hence undermine your credibility.

Eye contact with members of the audience is an important aspect of presentation. It is necessary for two reasons: credibility and inclusion. If you fail to establish eye contact with certain members of the audience they will feel left out of the presentation. They may even subconsciously start fidgeting in their seats to attract your attention.

Television producers know the importance of eye contact with the audience — that's why presenters are told to look straight down the barrel of the camera. This gives the viewer, who could be one of millions, the distinct impression that the person on television is speaking directly to them.

When lawyers address a jury, they attempt to generate the impression that they are looking into the jurors' souls through their eyes. It is difficult to persuade a jury not to sentence a man to life imprisonment if you don't look them directly in the eye when you tell them your client is innocent.

In maintaining eye contact, you need to be conscious of how long you focus on any one person at any one time. If you focus on one person for too long the rest of the audience will feel excluded, and that person may well become embarrassed by what they perceive to be an excess

Exhibit 4.2 *Hand gestures: (a) open hands on the crucifix; (b) test for rain; (c) 'light bulb point'; (d) 'fine thread extrusion'.*

of attention. On the other hand, glancing from person to person and failing to establish direct eye contact with anyone will not endear you to the audience. People with shifty eyes, whose gaze darts from one person to another, will be perceived as untrustworthy.

The appropriate length of time to look into any one person's eyes when speaking is generally about one and a half seconds. You should concentrate on moving your eyes from person to person, but you should not move your gaze too quickly.

Approaches to maintaining eye contact

Maintaining eye contact can seem to be a problem when you are speaking to more than one person. Whose eyes should you look at? When the Pope addresses the hundreds of thousands of assembled believers at the Vatican each Christmas, he cannot look them all in the eye. It is difficult to look even forty people in the eye. The question is: how do you generate the *impression* that you are looking everyone in the eye?

Uniform haphazard eye contact

One solution to this problem is the method called 'uniform haphazard eye contact'. The word uniform implies that you should seek to gain eye contact with each member of the audience (or section of the audience, if the audience is very large). No one should be excluded or overlooked.

The reason that your eye contact must be random is fairly plain. It would be possible to look everyone in the eye while speaking simply by shifting your eye contact from one person to the person next to them and so on. You could work your way through the audience, person by person, row by row. While this approach would be uniform, it would appear completely unnatural. You must be haphazard in the way you look around the audience.

The object of uniform haphazard eye contact is to

look into the eyes of every member of the audience in a random and unpredictable order.

Representative staring

Since individual eye contact with each member of a large audience is impossible, you should divide the audience into quarters in your mind: front left, front right, rear left and rear right. You should choose some point to mark the boundaries between each quarter. An aisle is often the best boundary. This approach is termed 'representative staring'.

When using this technique, you should still adopt the uniform haphazard approach to eye contact, moving your gaze from one quarter to another in a random fashion. Each quarter of the audience needs to feel equally included. This may be achieved by staring at each quarter of the audience for roughly the same amount of time throughout your speech.

It is crucial that within any one quarter, your gaze is evenly distributed. The representative staring approach will not be successful if, when looking in the third quarter, you always look at the same person. It is important to try to distribute your gaze over all four quarters evenly and within each quarter evenly.

For representative staring to work well, it is only necessary that you divide the audience into sections; they need not be divided into quarters if that would be inappropriate. For instance, if the aisles in the room naturally divide the audience into five groups, it would be a waste of time and effort not to use those existing divisions. However, in these situations you must remember to look at the front of each section as well as the rear.

Who to look at and who to avoid

There are a few techniques that are useful for fine tuning your eye contact. Don't waste your gaze on someone who is not looking at you. Similarly, it does little for your

Exhibit 4.3 *Get the audience in your sights and divide into quarters*

confidence as a speaker to spend time glaring at someone in the audience who is asleep. This will only increase any nervousness you may be feeling.

Remember that you must actually look at an audience, even when it is large. Speakers who look over the heads of the audience members are ineffective. They appear to be looking at the picture on the back wall or the light hanging from the roof rather than at the audience. Often this is a result of nervousness or inexperience — the speaker knows to look up but cannot bring themselves to look at a member of the audience.

Other 'problem' speakers look down at the ground or around the room. They are not looking at their notes, but because of nerves, they are not looking at the audience either. This often occurs in meetings, where the speaker fixes her gaze on something on the desk or table in front of her, or looks out the window while speaking. This is not inclusive and therefore not likely to be effective.

The solution for those who look anywhere but at the audience is a simple one. If you cannot bring yourself to look someone in the eye, look at the bridge of their nose. If you fix your stare just to one side of their nose, near their eyes, then you will not have to hold their gaze and be intimidated by them, but you will looking directly at people.

This device is perfect for the child being disciplined by their parent, who yells, 'Look me in the eye when I talk to you'. No one will find it easy to look into the eyes of someone who is screaming at them, but looking at a point near their eye provides a solution to this problem. This can also be a useful technique during interviews.

Using visual aids

As part of a presentation you will often find it useful to use overheads or slides, particularly if you are presenting numerical data. Graphs and charts can often convey data far more effectively than you can orally.

Look at the chart on page 108, a break-even chart. You can see that this chart shows a complex set of relationships in a much clearer way than you could with words alone. To explain this in words you might say something like:

This company will break even (on a cash basis) when the volume of sales is 100 units, assuming current prices and margins are maintained.

As can be seen, at less than 100 units, revenue is less than total costs. At more than 100 units, the company is making a profit.

The diagram explains the situation far more clearly than the oral explaination.

Combining an oral and visual presentation can be a significant challenge. When giving a presentation using visual aids, it is important to remember that the visual aids are merely meant to add to what you are saying. Too many people seem to see their role as providing waffle in between the charts, which they believe contain the message.

While charts can be useful, never use them as a substitute for oral communication. *You* should be presenting your story; the charts should just help you make some of the points more clearly. Hundreds of charts are almost always unnecessary. Usually a few charts, that clearly present some of the key material, are all that it takes. A few backup charts, with more detailed financial or other data, do not hurt if you have the time.

For instance, you might take an approach along these lines:

Over the last two months, as we all know, revenue has been declining alarmingly. Our analysis now indicates that most of this has been caused by a dramatic fall in sales revenue from widgets. **[Put up revenue versus time chart for widgets.]** As this chart shows, revenue

Exhibit 4.4 *Break-even chart*

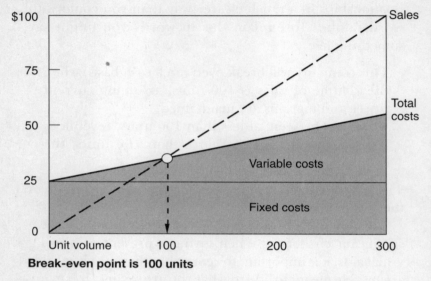

Dollar volume

Break-even point is 100 units

Source: Judy Marcus, *Communication Dynamics,* Self-published, Greenwich USA, 1980

from widgets has almost halved over the last two months. The reason for this decrease in revenue was that our major customers took only half as much stock as usual. Instead they have begun purchasing our rival's 'Schlock'. **[Put up chart of sales of widgets and schlock.]** As this chart shows, our volume decreased dramatically over the period, while Schlock volumes increased by more than 150 per cent.

The advantage of using charts is that they can make a concept not only easier to understand, but also easier to remember. Of course, it is important to choose the right charts. Although not dealt with in detail here, you need to be aware that there are right and wrong ways to present material. You don't just choose the type of chart based on aesthetic principles or personal taste.

As a basic guide, to show the size of items in relation to one another, use a *bar chart*. To show change over time, use a *column* or *line chart*. Use a *pie chart* to show the relative size of parts in relation to the whole. (See Exhibit 4.5)

All too often, people devalue excellent oral communication with a shoddy visual presentation. If you are going to show charts, it is worth making them look as professional as you'd like to sound. There are a number of software packages that can help you develop quality charts quite easily on your computer.

Avoid relying on your notes

The biggest down-side of using notes when communicating is the tendency to become dependent on them. Often people read their speech word for word, sometimes with stage directions included. It is important that your presentation does not merely consist of reading out a set of prepared remarks. If that's all you are going to do then you may as well hand out copies of your presentation and allow the audience to read it themselves.

As we discussed earlier, maintaining eye contact with the audience is a crucial part of any presentation, and for that reason you should only briefly glance at your notes. It helps if you don't write out your whole speech — all that should be necessary is a few key points to remind you of your direction (see Chapter Three). If you do write out your remarks in full, you may well fall into the trap of reading your speech word for word.

There are two key reasons why you should never read a speech. The first is that it reduces your ability to make the speech sound interesting. People who read their speeches are unable to use the techniques for effective presentation discussed in this chapter because they have to expend too much of their energy and concentration on reading the text of the speech.

Exhibit 4.5 *Standard charts*

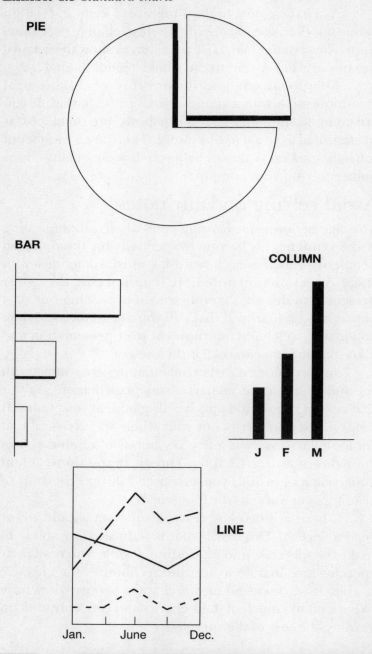

PIE

BAR

COLUMN

J F M

LINE

Jan.   June   Dec.

This hugely reduces the credibility of their speech. The impact of Martin Luther King's speech to the assembled throng in Washington would have been weakened had he read to them: 'I have a dream that one day this [*pause while he turns the page of his speech*] nation will rise up and live out the true [*pause while he tries to decipher his own handwriting*] meaning of its creed'. It is impossible to sound as convincing and as passionate when you are reading from notes as when you are speaking from the heart, albeit prompted by notes.

The second reason you should never read a speech has to do with flexibility. Any interruptions or questions asked by the audience can fatally interrupt the flow of your speech. It can be very difficult to return to the correct point in your speech if you are interrupted with a question or if someone interjects. An attack of nerves can have a similar effect. You may lose your place and become flustered. Speakers who rely on their notes are thus not only less effective presenters, they are also much less flexible in their presentation.

Used well, your notes should provide a reference point to which you can easily return if interrupted. They should free you to be more flexible and responsive, particularly in answering questions.

BUILD RAPPORT WITH YOUR AUDIENCE

Personal stories

Personal stories can be used to build rapport with the audience and to provide a 'human face' to any presentation. They can help you appear honest and open, and disarm the audience by personalising your message. But telling personal stories requires a delicate touch. They can be very useful in a range of contexts, but are also fraught with hazards.

One of the advantages of stories about your life is that they are easy to tell. You're unlikely to forget the ending or a punch line. Telling a personal story can also be a good way to relax and relieve stress.

At the same time, you need to be wary. Telling too many personal stories can appear self-indulgent and self-serving. Furthermore, they may be inappropriate in certain contexts. While they will often be suitable for an after dinner speech or an 'armchair' kind of speech (a general philosophical discussion in a relaxed, usually social, setting), personal tales may be somewhat out of place in a boardroom. When time is really of the essence, anything that strays off the point can reduce your impact.

Self-deprecation

Indulging in a degree of self-deprecation can also be an effective way of building rapport with the audience. If you are speaking to a foreign audience, then depending on cultural practice, it may be useful to make a joke about your accent or country of origin. Similarly, jokes about some other identifying feature can be used to relax and engage an audience.

However, there is a fine line between self-deprecation and excuses and apologies. Never apologise because you are not an experienced speaker or the world's foremost expert on a particular subject. The audience won't expect you to be the World's Best Speaker or a Nobel Laureate. However if you issue too many excuses and disclaimers, the audience will begin to lose confidence in you.

KEY POINTS

Style of speech
- No particular style is to be preferred
- Everyone can improve — speaking well is not an inherited ability
- Everyone needs to communicate well, not just public speakers

Manner of delivery
- Use appropriate language for the context
- Choose your words carefully
- Aim for clarity and use plain English
- Adopt a suitable volume, speed and tone
- Humour can be useful, but don't overuse it or feel that you have to be funny
- Repetition can be an effective means of emphasis

Visual presentation
- Maintain eye contact
- Gestures should add to your message, not detract from it
- Visuals should never be distracting
- Visual aids can help make complex points simple
- Avoid relying on your notes

Build audience rapport
- Use personal stories where appropriate
- Self-deprecation can disarm an audience

CHAPTER FIVE

HOW TO WIN ARGUMENTS

Show me a good loser and I'll show you a loser
WALLACE 'CHIEF' NEWMAN, COLLEGE FOOTBALL COACH,
TO A YOUNG RICHARD M. NIXON

Some people choose to argue, others find arguments thrust upon them. Arguments, plainly, are not just the province of the argumentative. Even the most committed pacifists will occasionally need to argue to defend their views against criticism.

Like many people, we enjoy a good argument — it is a great opportunity to really thrash ideas around and test your wits against your opponent's. Thus we came to compete at debating tournaments.

When we unexpectedly found ourselves in the Grand Final of the World Debating Championship in Princeton, New Jersey, we knew that we would have to do something special to beat the brilliant team from Oxford University.

When we won the coin toss we had the option of choosing which side we wanted. We already knew that the topic was 'That the right to life cannot be abridged', which we thought could potentially lead to a debate about one of three subjects: the death penalty, euthanasia or abortion.

We thought about the possibilities and chose the negative side. Not because we preferred the negative of any of those subjects, but simply because empirical evidence shows that in the United States the negative team more often wins finals. We went with the numbers.

We then had an hour to prepare for the final. Rather than briefly preparing for every possible subject that the Oxford team could choose to address, we put ourselves in their shoes. We thought that they would almost certainly choose to debate the death penalty. Arguing against the death penalty would give them a very strong empirical case as well as emotive arguments. It would leave us with a difficult argument, and very little substantive evidence and emotional material to play with.

So, rather than trying to prepare for all possible issues, we made a strategic choice to prepare only the death penalty argument. Our rationale was simple. If the Oxford team chose euthanasia or abortion, we were comfortable about the arguments and could make up a case on the run. Since we were almost certain that they would choose to debate the death penalty, and since that presented far more difficulties for us, that was what we would prepare.

We then had to decide what to argue in the negative. There are traditionally four arguments in favour of the death penalty:

1. It is cheaper than the alternatives
2. It is a more severe punishment than the alternatives
3. It prevents the criminal committing any more crimes
4. It is a better deterrent than the alternatives.

Generally, the approach that negative teams take is to argue that for these four reasons, the death penalty should be introduced (or retained, depending upon the state of the law at that time and place) for the usual range of heinous crimes. We were very conscious, however, of not trying to prove too much. We knew that we had to decide *how much we wanted to prove*.

First we decided that these four reasons were not all strong enough to argue. The first reason was patently untrue. With all the appeals that are allowed, putting someone to death is usually more expensive than keeping them in gaol for life. So we decided to ditch that rationale; we had to, since not only was it untrue, but everyone *knew* that it was untrue.

We also decided not to argue the second reason. This, we decided, was too subjective and likely to confuse the debate. It is very difficult to prove that one punishment is more severe than another.

Further, we decided not to press the third reason very strongly. This was partly because few criminals escape from maximum security prisons, so it was somewhat of a moot point, and also because we wanted to try to divert discussion away from the standard anti-death penalty argument, which is that once you have put someone to death there is no undoing it if you later find that you made a mistake.

In the end we decided to base our argument on the fourth point: that the death penalty is a deterrent in certain cases. The question this raises, of course, is: for which crimes should the death penalty apply? The fewer crimes for which we argued in favour of the death penalty, the easier our task. In the end we settled on four:

1. War crimes
2. Mass drug dealing
3. Serial killings
4. Murder of law enforcement officials.

This list may look a little arbitrary, but we wanted to focus on only a very limited number of situations in which the death penalty might apply. The fewer crimes for which we tried to prove that the death penalty should apply, the easier our task. As Exhibit 5.1 shows, the line we ended up taking only required us to prove a very narrow argument. Whereas the traditional pro-death penalty argument would have meant we had to 'win' in all 24 squares on the chart, we only aimed to win in four.

When the debate began, it was clear that the

Exhibit 5.1 *Narrowing the pro-death penalty argument*

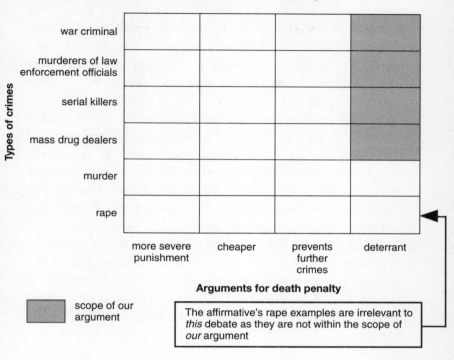

affirmative team was arguing against the death penalty, as we had assumed they would. They took the standard line, covering all four arguments in all types of crimes in which the death penalty is traditionally applied.

When it was time for us to speak, we demonstrated that the affirmative team's choice of the death penalty as a subject was unreasonable. Given that some pro-abortion doctors had recently been murdered in the United States, we argued that abortion was obviously what the debate was meant to be about and that the affirmative team had defined the topic self-servingly. The audience was on our side. They thought we were being treated unfairly, but that we were being good sports about it.

Next we showed that most of the affirmative team's

argument was irrelevant. They had argued that putting a rapist to death does not punish him any more than a life sentence, is not cheaper, and is inhumane. We could dismiss this argument as irrelevant because we weren't even arguing in favour of the death penalty for rape. The effect of our narrow negative was to make large parts of their argument only marginally relevant at best.

When all was said and said some more, we prevailed over the Oxford team in a six-five split decision. But had we taken the standard negative approach to the death penalty debate, the affirmative team would almost certainly have scored a resounding victory. Thinking strategically, rather than taking the typical knee-jerk reaction to the opposing argument, made all the difference.

In this chapter, we explain how to win arguments. Winning arguments is not just about being on the 'right' side, although that certainly doesn't hurt. A prerequisite for winning arguments is a clear vision of your objectives. That is, you need to be clear about what 'winning' really means.

APPROACHES TO WINNING ARGUMENTS

An argument is basically the clash of ideas. Sometimes arguments are amicable and friendly, sometimes aggressive and hostile. In any argument, the better view does not always prevail. There is a range of factors that will contribute to who wins, or is perceived to win, an argument. An argument is somewhat like politics, where the winner is rarely the smartest or most honest individual, but rather the person whose argument is more effective. An argument is not a quest for true pearls of wisdom, for perfect gems that no opponent will ever be able to fault. It is a contest of wits and wills.

Essentially, winning arguments is about the gentle

art of persuasion. You won't always be able to convince someone else of your point of view, but you should at least be able to reduce some of the distance between the two opposing views. Unsuccessful communication, on the other hand, can actually push people further away from your position. They may become even more entrenched in their belief that they are right and you are wrong. Be aware of the risks you take in getting into an argument.

There are a number of strategies that you can employ to make your argument more persuasive. Not all will be appropriate in every circumstance. Determining which of the following strategies you will adopt is a function of your precise objective and the context in which the communication is delivered.

In Exhibit 5.2 we have reproduced one person's advice on how to win arguments. We have seen these techniques used often, with varying degrees of success.

Exhibit 5.2 *How to win an argument*

I argue very well. Just ask any of my remaining friends. I can win an argument on any case, against any opponent. People know this and steer clear of me at parties. Often, as a sign of great respect, they don't even invite me. You too can win arguments. Simply follow these general guidelines.

Get drunk
Suppose you are at a party and some hot shot intellectual is expounding on the economy of Peru, a subject you know nothing about. If you are drinking some health-fanatic drink like tomato juice, you'll hang back, afraid to display your ignorance. But if you drink several jugs of beer, you'll discover you have strong views about the Peruvian economy. You'll argue forcefully, offering searing insights, and possibly upset

furniture. People will be impressed. Some may even leave the room.

Make things up

Suppose, in the Peruvian economy argument, you are trying to prove that Peruvian workers are underpaid, a position you base solely on the fact that you're underpaid and you'll be damned if you're going to let a bunch of Peruvians be better off than you are. Don't say, 'I think Peruvians are underpaid'. Instead say, 'The average Peruvian's salary in 1996 dollars adjusted for the revised tax base is $1,452.81 per annum, which is $887.24 below the mean poverty level'. (Note: always make up exact figures.)

If an opponent asks for the source of your information, make that up too: 'This information comes from Dr Hobel J. Moon's study for the Burford Commission, published February 1996. *Didn't you read it?* (Say this last bit in the same tone you would use to say, 'I stopped pulling the wings off bugs when I was three, didn't you?')

Use weighty sounding words and phrases

Memorise this list:

- Let me put it this way
- In terms of
- Vis-a-vis
- Per se
- Qua
- So to speak

You should also commit to memory some keen Latin expressions such as *QED*, *ipso facto* and *id est*. These all mean, 'I speak Latin and you do not'.

Here's how to use these phrases. Suppose you want to say, 'Peruvians would like to be able to buy expensive items like VCRs, but they don't have much money'. You would never win an argument speaking like that. But you will if you say, 'Let me put it this way, vis-a-vis Peruvians qua Peruvians, they would like to be able to purchase them, so to speak, but they do not have the purchasing power per se, as it were, QED'. Only a fool would challenge a statement like that.

Use snappy but irrelevant comebacks

You'll need an arsenal of all-purpose irrelevant phrases to fire back at your opponents when they come up with valid points. The best are:

- You're being defensive
- You're begging the question
- You're comparing apples and oranges
- You're stretching the range of your parameters.

(This last one is particularly valuable as no one short of a nuclear physicist has the vaguest idea of what parameters are.)

Here's how to use your comebacks. You say, 'Abraham Lincoln said in 1873 . . .'. Your opponent interrupts: 'Lincoln died in 1865'. You say, 'You're being defensive'.

So, that's it. Now you know how to out-argue anyone. Do not try to use these methods on people who are generally known to carry weapons.

Source: adapted from an anonymous source on the World Wide Web on the Internet.

How to prove an argument

Broadly speaking, you can prove an argument in two ways: from principle or by example.

To prove an argument from principle, you first need to establish the principle and then apply the facts to prove your point. For instance:

- 'Birds have wings and fly' — the principle that you are asserting
- 'An emu is a bird' — the facts
- 'Therefore the emu must be able to fly' — your application of the facts to the principle.

If there is real disagreement about your statement, it will centre on the principle. Some may question your assertion (or assumption) that *all* birds can fly.

To prove by example, on the other hand, you need to provide a number of examples which support your point and use them as the basis of your proof. For instance:

- 'Crows, eagles and owls are all birds; they all have wings and can fly' — your examples
- 'Therefore the emu, which is also a bird, must also have wings and be able to fly' — your conclusion.

In essence, what you are saying is: 'Here are three examples of birds that can all fly. Therefore the emu, which is also a bird, can also fly.'

The distinction between an argument from principle and an argument by example will not always be this obvious. Even when you are arguing from principle you will provide examples. Similarly, when arguing by examples you will draw some underlying principle from your examples.

When to argue from principle

Generally it is more effective to argue from principle when there are many counter-examples that can be made and you want to avoid what is described as 'example ping-pong'. For instance, if you are trying to argue that the Efficient Capital Markets Hypothesis is valid, you would probably be better off arguing from principle; there are simply too many examples that would undermine an argument by example. The argument from principle, however, is compelling; so compelling, in fact, that many economists still brazenly assert it as an obvious truth, notwithstanding the wealth of contrary empirical data.

When to argue by example

It is often more effective to argue by example when arguing from principle would be inconclusive and overly theoretical. For instance, if you are trying to prove that communism *cannot* work, and you choose to argue from principle, you would have to analyse the theory of communism to show that it is internally flawed and so cannot be successful, irrespective of how well it is applied in practice. This is a difficult argument and one that is likely to lead to an inconclusive and highly theoretical debate. In this case you might be better off arguing by example. In effect, you would base your argument on the fact that almost every significant communist regime has eventually failed, which shows that communism cannot work. Of course, your opponent could respond by arguing that the problem is in the application of communism rather than the theory, but that argument is fairly weak. You could then argue that if communism *could* work, at some point it *would have*.

How to refute opposing arguments

Refuting opposing arguments is a two-step process. First you need to isolate the issue, then you must give the grounds for criticism.

Isolate the issue

Isolating the issue is often a matter of intuition. It is the response that we automatically have when we hear something that is not quite right, or a little 'dodgy'. When someone says something to you that doesn't sound right, your next step is to isolate exactly what it is about the statement that you disagree with. You need to work out what it is that is untrue, unclear, incomplete, or contentious.

For instance, you might be arguing with someone

about whether democracy really works. Your opponent says it doesn't, and cites five examples which show that in the United States the Presidency is won by the candidate with the best campaign financing. You could choose to argue with each example, but if you isolate the issue you may be able to show a more fundamental flow — by basing the argument on the United States, your opponent is only considering one example of democracy. The issue is not just the US political system, but democracy as a form of government.

Grounds for criticism

There are six main approaches that can be taken to refute an opposing argument.

Error of fact

With this approach, you show that an opposing argument is based on factual error. For instance, someone may argue in favour of their son being given a senior job with his employer because he has ten years' experience in government employment. You point out that for the last ten years he has been collecting unemployment benefits, which is not quite the same thing as being in government employment.

Irrelevant argument

You may be able to show that your opponent's argument, while interesting, is irrelevant. For instance, you may propose that your company launch a new line of fruit juices, at which point someone argues against your proposition on the grounds that CFCs are damaging the ozone layer. You can refute this argument by showing that the production of the fruit juices won't produce any CFCs, so the argument is irrelevant.

Illogical argument

You may be able to argue that the conclusions being drawn

by the opposition do not flow logically from the facts presented. For instance, someone may argue against your being elected as president of the sailing club because you are a draft dodger who avoided serving in Vietnam. You could then point out that this criticism is illogical as you were only fourteen when the war ended and so you couldn't have served. You might further argue that the point is irrelevant as your war record has nothing to do with your suitability for the position.

Unacceptable implications

When using this approach, you demonstrate that the opposition's argument has ramifications which are repugnant. For instance, if it is proposed that euthanasia should be legalised to save the community money on hospital beds, you could point out that while money would be saved, that is not an acceptable justification for letting people die (although there may be other justifications for euthanasia).

Not persuasive

Sometimes you may concede that the opposition's argument is correct, but show that it should be given little weight. For instance, opponents in an election may point out that a candidate took drugs as a teenager. You could argue that since the candidate was only using marijuana, it was thirty years ago, and he didn't inhale, the argument should be given little weight.

Internal contradiction

You may be able to refute opposing points by showing that there are internal inconsistencies in the opposition's argument. For instance, someone who smokes heavily but complains that he is being poisoned by pollution from a nearby factory is being hypocritical. Therefore you could argue that his point should be given little weight.

Subtly lead the audience to your conclusion

In certain situations you may find it preferable for the audience to reach a particular conclusion for themselves, rather than you having to spell it out for them. The principal reason for adopting this approach is that people are often more enthusiastic about a proposal in which they have participated, than one they have merely been presented to rubber stamp. You can use this approach to build agreement and obtain 'buy-in' from the key participants.

A subsidiary benefit of subtly leading an audience to a particular conclusion is that it prevents blame being placed at your feet if there are negative consequences in the future. For instance, if a committee decides to adopt an approach to which you have subtly led them, then responsibility for that approach will rest with the whole committee. A risky plan will not be known as 'Bronwyn's solution', despite the fact that you were the instigator. This procedure is suitable when there is a strong likelihood that scapegoats may be sought at some future date. The drawback, of course, is that if the proposal is dramatically successful you may have difficulty taking the credit, but that's the nature of a trade-off.

The best approach when using this strategy is to make the key points in support of a particular conclusion and then leave it up to the audience to join the dots. For instance, show that the animal that was found has gills, swims in the water, is scaly and has a tail. Leave the audience to come to the startling conclusion that the animal must be a fish.

Doctors sometimes use this approach. Instead of advising you to take one option or another, they set both options out before you: 'You can either have a quite painless injection that will cure you rapidly, or we can do nothing for the moment, but you'll have to live with the green spots and nausea for a few weeks while we wait to see if the symptoms subside.'

Another advantage of this approach is that it shifts the burden of proof. Rather than saying, 'I believe that the animal that was found is a fish and here's my proof', in effect you're saying, 'Here are the facts. You decide'. There is always a risk that when you set out to prove something, someone will try to derail you — this approach reduces that risk.

For instance, suppose you are in a meeting and you have presented enough evidence to show fairly convincingly that a particular course of action should be followed. One or two people are opposed and they demand complete proof. They say, 'So what if sales go down immediately after we show *that* advertisement. That could be a series of coincidences. How can you prove that the advertisement is actually *causing* our sales figures to decline?'. Unless you have conducted market research, it is probably very difficult to *prove* a causal relationship. The circumstantial evidence, however, is pretty strong. If you had simply presented the evidence — 'For the last three months' sales figures have declined immediately after we have screened the advertisement with the giant frogs' — people might have reached the obvious conclusion themselves, and it would have been much more difficult for someone to criticise your evidence and conclusions.

Another method of subtly leading your audience towards your conclusion is to delicately dispose of the alternative possibilities. In effect, you say: 'There are three possible answers to this question: A, B and C. Since A and B are wrong, the answer must be C'. By taking a much more subtle approach, you can lead the audience to believe that they worked out that the answer was C themselves.

This is an occasion when signposting is not a good idea. Rather than explaining your approach to the audience, you need to subtly argue against alternative propositions while appearing to remain neutral. In this way you give the audience the impression that you are merely giving a general description of the relevant issues. In doing so, however, you manage to mention various negative points about alternative views. If you really want to maintain an aura of objectivity, you will have to be careful not to overstate your point.

For instance, suppose there are three possible locations for a new plant: A, B and C. You believe that the plant should be located at location B. Each location has one major defect: A is zoned residential, B is most expensive, and C is in the middle of nowhere. To push B, you could say, 'I'll just give a brief precis of the options available . . . [talk briefly about each one]. Now, the two key issues to be considered are location and zoning . . .'. You will probably have to mention cost, but you can play down its significance and so lead the audience towards your conclusion.

Pre-empt arguments

Sometimes the only way to reach your objective is to forestall an argument that is developing. For instance, in the death penalty debate referred to earlier, it could be argued that putting a criminal to death is the best form of justice for the victim. The other side may say, 'As you argued, doing justice is fundamentally important. Surely, then, we cannot put people to death when there is a chance that we have made a mistake about their guilt.'

By 'railroading' an opponent, making their stance untenable or uncomfortable, you can prevent them taking a position that is contrary to yours. Suppose the principal of your daughter's school is complaining to you about what a disruption little Emma is, and how her future at the school is looking somewhat uncertain. At this point it is very important to jump in before he actually says that he is going to expel her, because after he has said that it will be hard for him to reverse his decision without losing face.

The best approach is to refer to some platitudinous speech that he has made on some previous occasion: 'Indeed, Mr Smith, we understand your point about Emma. She really has been a little highly strung recently. As you were saying only the other week, it is at times like this that we have the greatest challenge as parents and educators. It is our job to inspire and motivate young people to apply themselves to the task at hand and smarten up their act. Quite frankly, Mr Smith, we are so happy that she is under your care. At some other schools they wouldn't have the skill or foresight to help Emma come around. We really appreciate your taking the time to speak with us today and the time that you personally are spending on Emma's future.' Mr Smith may then find it difficult to expel Emma.

The power of concession

When the media discovers that a candidate for elected office has a 'skeleton in the closet', be it a past infidelity, a tax problem or a tendency to experiment with illicit substances, they have a field day. The candidate is criticised on two fronts: first, for whatever the skeleton is, and second, for their lack of integrity. Often the second issue is the more important. People are more dismayed that the candidate lied or covered up than by the fact that he made a mistake.

The power of concession is that it may actually enhance your credibility while at the same time blunting a weapon that could be used to hurt you. If the candidate concedes that he once paid his tax late, but that it was a mistake and he's been diligent ever since, then this mistake may not hurt him. He may even score points for his honesty and integrity.

There are three main reasons why you should make concessions:

1. It is honest to do so
2. Adverse facts will do less damage coming from you than from your opponent
3. It allows you to focus the argument on relevant issues.

When to concede

Deciding when to concede is simple: as early as possible. If you are going to make certain concessions do this as soon as you can. Remember, concession that comes from you is far less harmful than being exposed by an adversary. If you delay, they might find your weak points before you have a chance to declare them yourself. If President Nixon, for instance, had come clean about Watergate at an early stage, he may have avoided the scandal that led to his resignation.

It is far easier to play down the significance of a particular point you have conceded yourself than to try to justify and explain it after others have exposed it.

What to concede

Deciding what to concede is more difficult than deciding when to concede. The general principle is to concede all *facts* that are detrimental to your argument. For instance, if you are arguing that your company should start selling a new flavour of bubble gum and the market research shows that most people dislike the flavour, you should concede this fact. Failing to do so would be dishonest. In conceding this you have an opportunity to provide an explanation. For instance, you might believe that the research is flawed because most of the people surveyed were over fifty whereas your target market consists of teenagers.

By making this concession you are, most importantly, safe-guarding your integrity. You also gain the subsidiary advantage of bolstering your credibility because you are seen to be frank, honest and open. Furthermore, you remove the risk of later exposure, at which stage things become very difficult to explain.

While you should concede *facts* that are contrary to your case, you should seldom concede *arguments* that are against you. For instance, in the previous example, if one argument that you have thought of *against* the new flavour is that consumers might be put off by the availability of too many flavours, there is no need to concede this point. If it is raised at a later stage, then you may indicate that it is a possible outcome or you may choose to provide counter-arguments. In either case, there is no need to concede the argument at the outset.

Help opponents save face

One of the secrets of effective communication is that you can often achieve your objective by helping others save face.

For instance, we were once trying to get a motion passed at our local sailing club to allow a new class of yacht to compete in races. One very influential member of the committee was opposed to the idea. He had already told a few of the committee members that he was opposed, but had yet to speak publicly to the members. We knew that we had to get him on side to get our motion passed. First, we approached him privately. We explained our case. We soon realised that he was not really opposed at all. He had misunderstood our position, believing that we wanted to introduce this class as a *substitute* for another class, rather than as an *additional* class. We suggested to him that he explain to the other committee members that he had had some concerns about the proposal but that we had been willing to address those concerns and reach a compromise. On that basis, he was now prepared to support the proposal, which was then passed unanimously.

We have seen so many cases, particularly in business contexts, where the principal impediment to the *right* decision being taken is that a senior executive has made too many statements opposing that decision in the past and so is forced to stick to her guns to avoid embarrassment.

In one particular instance, a new product was proposed, one which clearly made sense for the company. A senior executive with great influence strongly opposed it, because he had vetoed the proposal two years ago when it was first presented. If it was adopted now, he would look foolish. The person presenting the proposal this time around should have been more sensitive to this. He could have helped the senior executive avoid losing face by putting a great deal of emphasis on the changed circumstances. He could have strongly implied that two years ago would have been the wrong time to introduce the product, but now was the right time. He failed to do this, however, and so the senior executive once again succeeded in sinking the proposal.

There are two key points to keep in mind when helping people save face:

1. Try to prevent public statements disagreeing with you. Once someone has taken a position publicly, it is very difficult for them to back down without losing face.

2. Create the impression that you have compromised to get them to agree. That way they will not look as if they backed down. Rather, it will seem as though you saw the merit of their view and modified your proposal accordingly.

Don't prove more than you have to

Take the narrow path

In the story about the death penalty debate at the beginning of this chapter, you may have noticed that we did not actually argue all that much in the final. A number of people came up to us after the debate and said they thought we had taken a pretty soft line, in that we only argued for the death penalty in a very narrow set of circumstances.

They were right. But the reason we did that was because we had learnt the hard way. After years of trying to prove the laws of physics simply to show that water is wet, we learnt *not to prove more than you have to*.

We once attended a Father's Association meeting at which the committee was deciding where to allocate funds for the year. One father was particularly keen for funds to be allocated to the school orchestra. All he wanted was about $5000. A considerable number of the other fathers agreed that the orchestra deserved the extra funds.

This man could have spoken about what a worthy endeavour the orchestra was, why it needed the money, what it would do with it, and shown that the Association could afford it. This would have been the most simple and effective approach. Instead, he decided to launch an attack on school sports. He argued that the children were wasting too much time playing sport and were not getting enough culture. He said that it was time to stop funding sport and start giving funds to the arts. He didn't really care about whether or not the various sports were allocated funds, he just got carried away.

Since most of the fathers were keen sports fans, even those who would have been in favour of funding the orchestra were turned against his argument. In the end, no one voted for his proposal and the orchestra got nothing. By trying to prove too much, he alienated his audience.

Similarly, when some people ask their boss for a pay rise, they try to paint such a positive picture of themselves that she wonders whether they are asking to be appointed chairman of the board. She is so annoyed by this, she refuses the pay rise.

A far better approach is to work out carefully what you will have to prove to get the raise you want:

• you are doing a great job (with examples)

- you have taken on new responsibilities
- it has been a year since last pay rise (with inflation)
- your peers have been given pay rises.

As long as you don't try to prove too much, you will probably be successful.

Big red balls

Imagine you have been asked to prove that a particular object is not a big red ball. You could try showing that its colour is not red, its size is not large, and it is not shaped like a ball. If you succeed in these arguments, then you will have proven that it is not a big red ball.

However, your task is really much easier than that. You have a choice. You can either show that:

- it is not big; or
- it is not red; or
- it is not a ball.

You do not have to prove (or disprove) each element. You can simply choose the easiest one. If it is blue, for instance, then obviously it is not a big red ball. If you can easily show that the object is blue, you do not need to bother about showing that it is not big or not a ball.

Sometimes, to be on the safe side, you will want to argue all three elements. In case people do not accept your argument that it is not red, you will also argue that it is not big. If they reject that as well, you can still triumph if you succeed in persuading them that it is not a ball.

The 'big red ball' strategy is useful because it helps you to focus on your strengths and pick the gaps in an opposing argument. For instance, if you are pulled over by the police in the early evening for driving without lights, you could have four potential arguments:

1. I was not driving
2. It was not dark

3. My lights were on
4. I made a mistake but please let me off.

You do not need to prove all four points. If you succeed in proving only one, then you will avoid a ticket. If you try to prove all four, by the time you get to the fourth point the police officer is likely to be so fed up that he will also book you for causing a nuisance. On the other hand, if you know that you are in the wrong, you might be best served by going straight to argument number four. It is a long shot, even for a highly effective communicator, but possibly worth a punt.

Choose your words carefully

Whenever you communicate, your choice of words can make the difference between success and failure. The words you use not only convey your message, they also create the tone and mood. When you want to be 'upbeat' and positive, you can help reinforce your message by using appropriate words. For instance, you could describe yourself as 'enthusiastic and excited' about a particular project rather than 'able to begin forthwith'. When you want to create a feeling that your work is based on teamwork, refer to 'we' rather than 'I', and use words that emphasise cooperation.

When you want to bring the audience closer to your view than that of your opponent, you can achieve this simply by using appropriate language. An effective method is to refer to your opponent in the third person as 'he', 'she' or 'them', or even 'he and people like him', while simultaneously referring to yourself and the audience as 'we'. This creates the impression that you and the audience are part of the same team, whereas your opponent is one of 'them'.

Word selection can also be used to help win the audience over to your point of view. For instance, if an earlier speaker has seemed pompous or arrogant, don't make the mistake of following his example. You may choose to subtly expose his pomposity, not by hitting the audience over the head — 'Hey, that guy was really pompous' — but rather by using a contrasting approach. If you use less formal language and adopt a more relaxed demeanour, you will shine in contrast to the earlier speaker.

Similarly, if an earlier speaker has been rude or arrogant, you can set an example by being far better mannered. If she referred to former President George Bush as 'George', you can make a point of referring to him as 'President Bush'. If she swore or used inappropriate language, you can subtly point that out: 'Miss Stewart mentioned that she did not believe that current Managing Director was performing adequately, although I think that she used a more colourful expression.' In this way you can lift yourself above the gutter approach of your adversary.

Whatever the situation, you should always try to stand out from the speaker immediately before you by adopting a vocabulary and tone that contrasts with their approach — even if you agree with them. By doing so, you can make it easier for the audience to concentrate on what you're saying. The change and variety may kindle new interest in the audience and enhance their attention span.

Use a contrasting approach

Contrast can also be used strategically in other situations. Whenever you are called upon to speak after someone else, you need to consider the best way to make yourself stand out from that person. If they have shouted throughout their speech, then you should start your speech in a much quieter voice. If they have spoken in a quiet and nervous voice, then you should start in a louder and more confident voice. Similarly, if they have been slow, mumbled, and left long pauses, then you should start your presentation with a burst of energy.

The use of a contrasting approach makes it possible for you to turn an opponent's strength into a comparative weakness. If they have told a string of jokes, then you should be wary of trying to out-joke them. It may be worth pointing out that the issue in question is a serious one, thus undercutting your opponent without personally attacking them. The approach is subliminal; the audience will enjoy the contrast.

We have used this tactic with some success during many debates at the World Debating Championship. Perhaps the best example was a debate against Harvard University on the subject: 'That women are now on top'. The Harvard team took a humorous line about women's sexual liberation. They made a few blue jokes that we supported with some risqué interjections. The first Harvard speaker began to feel confident that we would endorse his very light-hearted approach to the topic.

The successful undercutting occurred when we started to speak. We made it clear that the subject called for an examination of whether sexism was still alive and well. We suggested (in serious and earnest tones) that the prevalence of blue humour and sexual innuendo about women 'being on top' was proof that sexism was alive and well. We hijacked a humorous debate and made a firm lunge for the moral high ground. In this context, our opponents appeared to be male chauvinist pigs who were sexually unliberated. While this may (or may not) have been the case, we magnified the situation by undercutting them with our choice of language and approach.

Make your 'air time' count

Know when to speak up

At a strategy meeting of the top 50 executives of a Fortune 500 company, much discussion took place about the company's future direction. Over two days, everyone had their say in a series of presentations and free-for-all-discussions.

Some executives spoke often, some spoke for long periods, some spoke seldom. Two weeks later, when the chief executive was presenting a summary to the board, it was one particular woman who spoke least who ended up being quoted most often. Throughout the two-day discussion, she only spoke when she had something insightful to offer. When someone made an obvious mistake in calculating the cash flow, she remained quiet. She figured that someone else could point that out (which they did, believing that they would impress everyone with their financial and analytical ability). When she spoke, it was to offer a new perspective on the company's strategy; a view that had not been discussed previously. She spoke only briefly, but her comments had real impact.

This is not an isolated example. Often the best way to achieve the greatest impact is to speak only when you have something profound or compelling to add. Even then, speak only briefly. Conciseness will add clarity and weight to your point. Too many people believe that to achieve the greatest impact, they need to have maximum 'air time'. They believe that if there are ten people at a meeting and they get 30 per cent of the 'air time', then they are doing well. But they are wrong.

Those who speak most are often stating the blindingly obvious. Furthermore, they usually take three sentences to say something that could have been said in one. These people are frustrating to listen to and are annoying to meet with. They are unlikely to go far.

Know when not to speak

Knowing when not to speak is as important is knowing when, and how, to speak. There are certain circumstances in which you will vastly reduce your impact if you say anything at all. This is particularly the case when the situation has become heated and unnecessarily adversarial. For instance, you should try to not to enter into personal slanging matches. If someone tries to bait you by being insulting, turn the other cheek and do not respond. It is important to keep in mind the objectives that you have set for the communication. Rarely will your objectives be met by responding to an attack.

This approach is also incredibly frustrating to the person who is trying to bait you. There is nothing more annoying in an argument than someone who will not fire back. If you do not respond to their attacks, then you provide your opponent with far less ammunition with which to attack you. As soon as you make just one personal response, you have lowered yourself to their level.

Similarly, you should avoid entering into a heated argument that is taking place between other people. It is best to avoid the collateral damage that getting involved is likely to bring. Many people seem to enjoy taking on the role of peacemaker when hostilities erupt during a presentation or meeting. As the United Nations has often found, peacemakers tend to get quickly caught up in the dispute themselves. If you seek to intervene in an argument, one side will inevitably feel that you are out to get them. In the worst case scenario, both sides will reach this conclusion.

Therefore, in situations where your comment will not have a high impact, you are often better off saying nothing at all. The more you say, the more you will dilute your message. Pedantry should be left to pedants and nitpicking should be the province of nits.

Use disagreement to your advantage

Despite the fact that we advise you not to become involved in a dispute, on some occasions disagreement within a group will provide you with an opportunity to further your objective. When there is disagreement and confusion over a particular issue, you may be able to step in as the voice of reason to unite the warring parties and present your view as representing a consensus.

This requires some degree of finesse; it is of paramount importance that you don't get sucked into the mire of the disagreement. Always remain above an argument. Never let yourself become involved, except as an arbiter. For instance, suppose your local tennis club is considering resurfacing the courts. The club is fairly evenly divided: one group wants clay, the other wants artificial grass. Your game, however, is best suited to the current grass surface. The two camps are fiercely divided. You may be able to take advantage of the situation by suggesting that the club appoint a committee to investigate the options. Once you've bought time, you may be able to scuttle both ideas by subjecting the issue to endless discussion. After all, many good ideas die in committees.

Cast aspersions with a smile

There are very few contexts in which casting aspersions on those with whom you disagree will be effective or appropriate. Generally it will be unnecessarily confrontational and aggressive. But although personal attacks should be avoided, at times they are acceptable; for instance, in a very informal setting, where no one will take great offence, or when describing an opponent at a political rally. Personal attacks on people who disagree with you are seldom appropriate, but there are effective ways of casting aspersions with a smile in an acceptable and reasonable manner.

Some speakers like to use the backhanded approach: 'I don't think Jim is stupid . . . but, plainly, whoever wrote his speech today is a blithering idiot'. This is not advisable. It is too obvious and you are likely to look foolish.

There are more subtle ways to cast aspersions. For

instance, you can subtly cast aspersions on a person's motives. Often this is simply a matter of reminding the audience of logical connections that already exist but that they may not have noticed. Suppose Jim has just presented a passionate argument about why the widgets unit should not be closed — directly after your presentation, in which you argued that it should be closed. You may be able to undermine Jim's argument by saying: 'Jim raised some very interesting points, which I'd like to address. Jim is particularly well placed to understand the position of the widgets unit, given that his team spends 90 per cent of their time doing maintenance on the widget plant. However, I believe that some of the arguments raised are outweighed by the evidence I presented previously . . . '.

In this example, you are apparently praising Jim's arguments and saying that he is in a good position to know what's what. But what you're actually saying is, 'Remember that Jim has a very strong vested interest in retaining the widget plant; if it goes, he loses his job'.

Undermine your opponent's credibility

Sometimes you can attack an opponent's argument simply by undermining their credibility. In sporting circles, this is referred to as 'playing the man not the ball'. It is a strategy often used by the politician, journalist and stand-up comic. Of course, it won't be appropriate in many situations, so use it sparingly.

The key to this approach is that the credibility of an argument or statement is inherently linked to the credibility of the person delivering it. By 1975, following the Watergate scandal, Richard Nixon could have told you that water is wet and that the sky is blue and you would not have believed him since his credibility had been dramatically undermined by the liberal American news media. On the other hand, at his peak, Mahatma Ghandi could have convinced you of virtually anything. Such was his credibility and reputation as an honest man.

'Playing the man not the ball' is common in everyday life. Young children often respond to criticism from one of their peers with a retort such as 'Your mother wears army boots' (or something even more crass). The child's response has nothing to do with the merits of the argument; it is a personal attack. Similarly, at meetings people sometimes accuse others of missing the point or being defensive. This has nothing to do with the issues; once again, it is a personal attack.

For best effect, personal attacks or attempts to undermine your opponent's credibility should be either *subtle*, such as 'You're right and I'm wrong, as you usually are', or *witty*, such as when someone is described as 'the kind of person who takes two hours to watch *60 Minutes*'. The 'iron fist in the velvet glove' best typifies the approach that you should use when attacking a person rather than their argument. If you can subtly undermine someone's intelligence, diligence or integrity, you may be able to demolish aspects of their presentation that have little to do with these attributes while still keeping the audience on your side. Alternatively, the retort 'What would you know? Your breath stinks!' is hardly likely to win friends and influence people.

Undermining your opponent's credibility can be a useful strategy if your opponent makes some factual errors which do not, however, detract much from their point. In this situation you may be able to undermine their whole argument simply by pointing out that they have not been rigorous in their presentation of certain facts. If they are wrong about X , they may be wrong about Y and Z as well, or so the argument goes. The impression that you are trying to convey to the audience is that your opponent is wrong on one issue because they were too casual with the facts and is therefore the kind of person who could be wrong about other issues. You introduce doubt as to your opponent's credibility, and thus imply that the audience should not believe anything else your opponent has said.

This technique is very similar to that of the lawyer who exploits the dubious credibility of a witness by suggesting to the jury: 'If he lied about that, then why should we believe him now?' or, 'She was wrong about the time of the explosion, so how can we be certain that she actually saw my client running away with a rocket launcher?'. In the legal world, this approach is called 'attacking the credit of a witness'. It involves an attack on their perception, memory, precision and/or intelligence.

Another effective method of undermining the credibility of an opponent can be to raise doubts about the methodology they have used and the assumptions they have made as a result. This can make their whole argument seem suspect. A good example of this approach is the debate that followed the release of *The Bell Curve* by Hernstein and Murray. This book, in part, sought to analyse the relationship between race and IQ. Critics of the book attacked it on the basis that it was racist. While the authors went to considerable lengths in the book to establish their findings as the logical conclusion of their empirical research, the attacks were in large part successful because of the contentious subject matter discussed in the book and the divisive findings. The conclusions were rarely debated on their merits and the two authors were widely vilified. The idea that was planted in the mind of the public was that the authors set out to make certain findings to support their elitist and racist hypothesis.

Undermining your opponent's credibility can be a very successful technique if used effectively, but it can have horrendous consequences if performed inexpertly. It will often be inappropriate and can turn the audience against you if it looks as though you are starting a fight. Personal attacks can also seem grubby and cheap. If the victim of the attack is perceived to be weak by the audience, then the personal attack can seem vicious.

There is a fine line between undermining an opponent's credibility and appearing to be a pedant. For instance, if someone is arguing that nuclear weapons should never be used, and that the United States was wrong to drop the bomb on Hiroshima, but says that the bomb was dropped in 1946 (rather than in 1945), their mistake is essentially immaterial. It does not change the argument. If you try to disagree with their point on the basis that they got the year wrong, you may look like a petty point scorer. At the same time, however, even minor factual errors can sometimes undermine someone's credibility with the audience. The audience may think, 'If that guy is such an expert on nuclear warfare, how come he doesn't even know when the bomb was dropped on Hiroshima? Maybe he's just talking out of his hat'.

If you decide to try to use this technique, it is important that you do so subtly and not offensively. Don't risk turning a civilised, reasonable debate into a personal slanging match.

Take risks

Winning arguments sometimes requires doing more than just putting forward the safe, conservative case that no one is likely to disagree with. You may have to take risks in order to achieve your objective. For instance, if you are one of ten thousand applicants for an exciting job in advertising, then there is no point sending in a 'Dear Sir/Madam' letter. The odds are dramatically against you, so you really have nothing to lose by taking a risk. The same is true of oral communication. To win an argument, sometimes you will need to go out on a limb.

You need to make a strategic choice about what you are trying to achieve with your communication. Sometimes a 'crash' or 'crash through' approach makes sense, where you either fail miserably or win gloriously. This was the view taken by Hugh Gallagher when he applied to New York University. He knew that he was not an outstanding scholar, but he believed he could demonstrate that he had the necessary flair and imagination to be a successful student.

His application, which we have reproduced in Exhibit 5.3, is a brilliant example of thinking outside the box. He was admitted to NYU because his application plainly demonstrates an exceptional capacity for creative thinking.

This application shows an excellent understanding of how to win an argument by taking a risk. It is the type of application that you either love or hate. If the wrong people read it, Hugh was out. For Hugh there was little risk. He had nothing to lose, because if he had put in a traditional application he would almost certainly have been rejected. He knew that the only way he would win the argument over whether he should be admitted to NYU was to go out on a limb.

If, on the other hand, Hugh had had fantastic marks and a great résumé, then submitting this application might have been somewhat unwise. After all, why take a risk when you don't need to?

Exhibit 5.3 *Living on the edge*

The University sought an essay response from each applicant answering the question: 'Are there any significant experiences you have had, or accomplishments you have realised, that have helped to define you as a person?'

'I am a dynamic figure, often seen scaling walls and crushing ice. I have been known to remodel train stations on my lunch break, making them more efficient in the area of heat retention.

I translate ethnic slurs for Cuban refugees. I write award-winning operas. I manage time efficiently. Occasionally, I tread water for three days in a row. I woo women with my sensuous and godlike trombone playing, I can pilot bicycles up severe inclines with unflagging speed, and cook Thirty-Minute Brownies in 20 minutes . . .

Using only a hoe and a large glass of water, I once single-handedly defended a small village in the Amazon Basin from a horde of ferocious army ants.

I play bluegrass cello. I was scouted by the Mets; I am the subject of numerous documentaries. When I'm bored, I build large suspension bridges in my yard. I enjoy urban hang-gliding. On Wednesdays, after school, I repair electrical appliances free of charge.

I am an abstract artist, a concrete analyst and a ruthless bookie. Critics worldwide swoon over my original line of corduroy evening wear. I don't perspire.

I am a private citizen, yet I receive fan mail. Last summer I toured New Jersey with a travelling centrifugal-force demonstration. My deft floral arrangements have earned me fame in international botany circles.

Children trust me. I can hurl tennis rackets at small moving objects with deadly accuracy. I once read *Paradise Lost*, *Moby Dick* and *David Copperfield* in one day and still had time to refurbish an entire dining room that evening.

I know the exact location of every food item in the supermarket. I have performed several covert operations for the CIA. I sleep once a week; when I do sleep, I sleep in a chair. While on vacation in Canada, I successfully negotiated with a group of terrorists who had seized a small bakery.

The laws of physics do not apply to me. I balance, I weave, I dodge, I frolic, and my bills are all paid.

On weekends, to let off steam, I participate in full-contact origami. I have made extraordinary four-course meals using only a mouli and a toaster oven. I breed prize-winning clams.

I have won bull fights in San Juan, cliff-diving competitions in Sri Lanka and spelling bees at the Kremlin. I have played Hamlet, have performed open-heart surgery and I have spoken to Elvis.

But I have not yet gone to college.

Source: adapted from an anonymous source on the World Wide Web on the Internet.

KEY POINTS

Pre-empt arguments
- Avoid arguments that you don't need to have. Sometimes you can get to your objective by *avoiding an argument*

Don't prove too much
- Only prove as much as you need to reach your objective — don't fight battles for the thrill of it

Concede early
- You will minimise the damage of adverse facts by conceding them early

Subtly lead the audience to your conclusion
- You can often lead the audience to your conclusion by drawing the dots and letting the audience connect them

Help opponents save face
- By helping opponents save face you will remove a significant impediment to their coming round to your view

CHAPTER SIX

ASK AND ANSWER QUESTIONS EFFECTIVELY

*Ask an impertinent question and you are
on the way to the pertinent answer*
J. BRONOWSKI, *THE ASCENT OF MAN*

Being able to ask and answer questions effectively is an important element in being persuasive. No one will succeed in proving their point if they are unable to answer questions about what they are saying. Many people are happy to give a speech or presentation, but find the prospect of having to answer questions quite terrifying. Questions can be unpredictable. Irrespective of how much preparation you do, there will always be a question you hadn't anticipated.

Questions, however, should be seen as an opportunity to interact with the audience. They enable you to gauge whether the audience is following you, understanding your argument and agreeing with what you say. If you can answer questions well, they will help you get your message across. In a job interview, for instance, the questions that you are asked give you an indication of what the employer is looking for, and your answers give you the chance to show that you will be able to do the job well.

Asking questions is also important. It helps you to stay involved when someone else is speaking. Questions can also be used to clarify and expand the key issues or to put forward a contrary view.

How to answer questions effectively

Being able to deal with questions well is as important as the substantive material that you present. For your communication to be effective, your listeners need to have any issues that they have with it resolved.

Be prepared

Being well prepared is crucial to answering questions well. Many questions can be anticipated with a bit of thought. There are certain generic questions that you should almost always have a response for in any business setting:

BENEFIT QUESTIONS
• What will we gain by doing this?
• What are the alternatives?
• What is the risk if we don't do this?

ACTION QUESTIONS
• What steps should we take to implement your ideas?
• Who will take responsibility for the project?
• How long will it take?

COST QUESTIONS
• How much will this cost?
• How much do alternatives cost?

A good approach is to get a group of people together around a whiteboard and brainstorm the issues that could come up and then prepare answers. Have back-up charts if necessary to answer the crucial, and obvious, questions.

If a question is predictable, such as those based on obvious weaknesses in your argument, you may decide to pre-empt it by answering it in advance. While this can sometimes be a good idea, to save interruptions and prevent any petty point-scoring, it is not always advisable. If you try to pre-empt questions too often, you may distract yourself from the key points that you are making.

It can often look very impressive when you have a 'killer' answer already prepared to a likely question. If you can rattle off a detailed answer to a difficult question, it will often enhance your credibility with the audience. Some people take this approach even further by deliberately setting out to prompt someone to ask a question to which they have a brilliant answer prepared. This can be effective, but requires great subtlety. You can look too clever for your own good if it becomes obvious. There are other risks as well. We have seen a speaker cleverly manipulate the audience until someone asked him the question to which he had prepared his 'killer' answer. At that point, however, someone else quickly popped up with the answer and was left to take the glory. The speaker looked somewhat foolish because most people assumed that he didn't know the answer.

Encourage questions

Answering questions can be quite daunting. After all, despite your preparation, you cannot be absolutely certain that you will always know the answers. Nonetheless, do not be afraid of questions, or seek to avoid them. Questions are important for three main reasons:

1. They dramatically increase an audience's attention span and level of engagement. It is like the difference between sitting through a two-hour lecture and being part of a two-hour discussion.

2. They allow you to deal with the audience's concerns about your communication and thus increase its effectiveness.

3. They help you build credibility and gain agreement on minor issues along the way.

You can encourage questions by saying up front that you are happy to answer questions at any time. Try to create a relaxed environment in which people are not afraid to ask questions. A good way to encourage questions is to pause for slightly too long after major points. People do not like the uncomfortable silence and are likely to be encouraged to ask a question.

Speak spontaneously

The ability to think quickly and speak spontaneously is fundamental to handling questions well. If you are asked a question that you have not previously considered, don't panic. Take a few moments to work out an answer. Answers do not have to be prepared. Be willing to think on your feet and adapt to changing circumstances.

Learn to listen

Whenever you are asked a question, always pause for a few moments before saying anything. Even if the question is blindingly obvious, wait a few seconds.

There are four reasons for this:

1. It allows you to concentrate entirely on listening to the question. This is crucial. Don't assume that you know what the question will be after the first three words. Certainly you should never interrupt someone by starting to answer a question that they haven't finished.

   You need to listen for both the content and the intent of the question. You need to understand both what is openly asked and what is hinted at but not said. Sometimes a question of fact will contain a subtle message. For instance, the question 'Where will the funding come from?' in some cases might be a subtle way of saying 'You must realise that we haven't got the money for this'.

2. A pause conveys the impression that you are a thoughtful individual who listens and thinks before speaking. Make sure you focus your eye contact on the questioner and give them your full attention.

3. A short pause demonstrates that you are giving the question due consideration. This is important because no one likes to think (or wants others to believe) that

they asked a stupid question. A quick reaction sometimes tends to give the impression that the answer was so obvious as to make the question unnecessary. A pause shows that you are taking time to think because it was a good question.

4. You can always use the time to think. Even if a question seems obvious, it is worth thinking about the best way of answering it. Try to find the words to answer it clearly, concisely and without snubbing the questioner. If the question was not entirely clear, sometimes it is a good idea to repeat a brief summary of the question before answering it. Alternatively, explain that you are not entirely clear about the question. Never blame the questioner, always take the responsibility yourself. You should say, 'Just to make sure that I understand the question properly, would you mind explaining . . . ', rather than, 'Your question was confusing. Please repeat it, but in plain English this time'.

Treat the questioner with respect

Always try to imply that a question was insightful and relevant, but avoid overusing phrases such as 'Good question' or 'I'm glad you asked that', as these stock phrases may make you seem patronising. Instead, you should deal with questions in a way that demonstrates the relevance of your answer by leading it back into the body of the presentation. Referring back to the question later is also a particularly effective way of reinforcing the value of the question. Remember, if people asking questions are made to feel that they are following your argument and engaging with you in an insightful way, they are more likely to agree with you and be impressed by your presentation.

Never avoid a question or put off your answer until later. If someone asks a question about something that you were planning to talk about later, make your point briefly and say that you will come back to the point in more detail later. Don't just say, 'I'll deal with that point later'. The questioner will feel snubbed. Furthermore, it will look as though you're ducking the question, or as though you're so inflexible that you cannot answer a question that comes out of order in your notes. There is also a chance that you won't return to that point at all because you get sidetracked somewhere else, and then it will really look as though you are avoiding the point.

If you don't know the answer to a question, then honesty is always the best policy. Don't make excuses; just admit it and move on. Promise to get back to the questioner with an answer, and make sure you do. This is a matter of basic politeness.

By admitting that you don't know the answer to a question, you don't necessarily detract from your credibility. In some respects you reinforce your credibility because the distinct implication is that you really do know about all the other material that you are discussing. Subconsciously the audience is thinking, 'She admits what she doesn't know, so what she says is probably true'.

If you try to bluff your way out of questions to which you don't know the answer, you will quickly erode your credibility. Invariably someone else will know the answer and will soon realise that you're just making it up. Don't take the risk. It's just not worth it. Once you have lost your credibility, you will have great difficulty regaining it.

Monitor the audience's response

You can tell a great deal about what an audience is thinking by their reactions. Most people's responses to your communication will be easy to read by watching their body language. They will nod their heads when they agree with you and frown or shake their heads when they disagree.

You need to watch your audience attentively, and try to understand what they are thinking. Do they agree or disagree? Are they interested and engaged? Are they listening? Are they even awake? If you notice someone frowning or shaking their head, it is an obvious sign that they did not understand your point, or that they disagree with what you are saying. Chances are that if they disagree, others might as well. You now have a great opportunity to have another go. Explain the point again, but this time make a particular effort to be clear and concise. Give an example or two if it will help. At the end of this, summarise. Pause for slightly too long. By creating a slightly uncomfortable pause you will make it easier for someone in the audience to ask a question, which might help you understand what the sticking point is.

Sometimes a member of the audience will use the opportunity to ask questions as a means of giving long and meandering speeches. As the audience becomes annoyed with the questioner, the responsibility will shift towards you to deal with the problem. Never be rude, but subtly shut the questioner out. Avoid catching their eye when they want to ask another question; if they look as though they're about to speak, you should keep speaking. Avoid long pauses. If necessary, offer to deal with their questions in private.

Get to the point quickly

We have already discussed the need to maximise the impact of your 'air time'. This also applies to answering questions. Once you have answered a question, stop. Don't feel you need to give a long soliloquy. Don't try to embellish a simple answer with detailed, irrelevant facts.

Keep to your agenda

When communicating with a group of people, be wary of getting caught up in a one-to-one argument. If one person asks you a question, be sure to deliver your answer to the whole group. Don't look only at your questioner, and don't look at them for approval when you've finished. To do so merely invites a one-on-one argument. Remember that you are addressing the entire audience — you cannot afford to be diverted to one person's issues or agenda.

Of course, if the incessant questioner happens to be your boss, or a key decision maker, then a different approach is needed. It is important to watch them closely and adapt your approach according to their reactions. When they ask a question, you need to be sure that they are satisfied by your answer. It may be to your advantage to involve them in an ongoing dialogue as this will allow you to be sure that you have addressed their concerns, and will help them feel that they have participated and been involved.

Types of questions

In general, there are three broad types of questions: empirical questions (questions which seek facts or information), questions of opinion and argumentative questions.

Empirical questions

Empirical questions are fairly easy to answer, assuming that you know the facts. If a questioner is genuinely seeking a fact, don't try to give them more. Sometimes, however, you will be unsure whether the question is simply a request for facts, or whether the questioner is trying to make a particular point.

For instance, someone might ask the question, 'I read in the papers that the plant will not be operational until 2006. Is that right?'. That could be a question of fact requiring you to answer 'Yes it is' or 'No, it will be ready in 2002'. Alternatively, it could be a criticism of the delay, in which case you could launch into a defence of your timetable. Generally, you should be wary of reading too much into a question. If you are asked a question of fact, then answer with facts. However, take note of any implications that you think are being made. If they are significant, you can address some of the concerns which seem to exist at a later point. For instance, five minutes after the question has been asked, you can explain the rationale for the timetable for the plant, without being defensive.

Questions of opinion

These questions can be difficult to answer. You should only express opinions when you feel comfortable doing so, not because you are tricked or forced into it by a question. There are a number of reasons why you may not want to express an opinion on certain issues. You may not have given the issue enough thought. Perhaps the issue is inherently uncertain (such as next year's profit), or requires knowledge of facts not available to you. In some cases, giving your opinion will unnecessarily expose you to controversy, particularly if you haven't had time to give the issue due consideration or find out what others may be thinking.

Avoid expressing opinions that you are not comfortable with. If you are asked to estimate profits for next year but would rather not, then simply say, 'I have not done that analysis'. If you do express an opinion, try to make your assumptions clear. For instance, 'I believe that profits will be up by 15–25 per cent next year, assuming that we introduce the cost-cutting measures that we have discussed today and that world pork belly prices continue to increase at their current rate'.

Argumentative questions

Sometimes a question will really be a statement or an argument. For instance, 'Have you ever actually been out to see one of these plants that you are such an expert on the finances of?' Never take the bait. Always keep your points simple and unemotional. By presenting clear, factual material, you will be able to disarm any emotive attacks or arguments, because the questioner and the audience will realise that you are not prepared to engage in an argument.

Argumentative questions pose particular difficulties, because you must answer the question but at the same time avoid conflict. In these cases it is often best to avoid reading between the lines. If there is a barb hidden in the question, simply ignore the barb. For instance, in reply to the question about whether you have visited the plants, simply answer politely: 'Yes, I have been fortunate enough to visit the plants on a number of occasions, and have found this very valuable. I'm hoping to get out there more often in the future.'

How to ask effective questions

There is no formula for asking effective questions. A 'killer' question will seldom have a yes/no answer or be a simple factual enquiry. Rather, it will be a question that really hits its mark and accomplishes its objective. A good question does not necessarily have to be one that is designed to fluster and confuse the recipient. Instead it will prompt the recipient, and others present, to consider a different angle or issue.

If you ask a question of a speaker giving a seminar or of someone at a meeting, you may have a number of different objectives. Sometimes you will simply be looking for a factual answer. You might want to know the exact monthly sales figures or the source material on which a particular statement is based. But think before you ask. Some people say that there is no such thing as a dumb question, but we all know that's not true. The *Salt Lake Tribune* once ran a series on the most stupid questions asked by lawyers in court, which included: 'The youngest son, the twenty-year-old, how old is he?'; 'Was that the same nose you broke as a child?'; 'Was it you or your brother who was killed in the War?' If you ask a dumb question, people will think less of you. You should also consider whether anybody else will be interested in your question. If there are fifty people in a room and you ask a question that could only be of interest to you, it might look somewhat self-indulgent. Be considerate.

Sometimes the objective of your question will be to embarrass or 'trip up' the recipient. Questions like this often start with 'Surely you're aware that . . . ' or 'Do you seriously deny that . . .'. These types of questions are seldom effective because they immediately let everyone know that you are picking a fight. A much more subtle and effective means of exposing the flaws in someone's argument is to sugar-coat the medicine. These questions often start with 'As you were saying . . . ' or 'I agree with that point and of course the corollary of that is . . .'. You begin by reinforcing the recipient's point and reassuring them that you are on their side. You then put a proposition to them which you know they disagree with, but which they will have difficulty rejecting.

On other occasions you may be trying to further a particular proposition. This is the 'statement-wrapped-up-in-a-question' question. For instance, 'That was also the case in 1960 when President Kennedy bought votes to win the presidential election, wasn't it?', is not really a question but a statement.

Asking effective questions requires careful thought about what you are trying to achieve. Key questions can help you achieve your objective, but remember that poorly thought out questions can undermine your credibility.

Exhibit 6.1 *Common objectives of effective questions*

Objective of question	Example
To expose inconsistency	Previously you've said X, but now you say Y. Which is it?
To expose factual errors	You've said that we made $X last year, but according to the Annual Report . . .
To articulate key issues	So what it boils down to is . . .
To expose lack of preparation	Surely you've read last week's report which discusses this point in detail?
To expose vested interest	Don't you own 20 per cent of the company that you're proposing we take over at a 100 per cent premium?
To articulate counter-arguments	On the other hand, couldn't it be said that . . . ?
To articulate a clear summary	So the key points are . . . ?
To clarify outstanding concerns	So the main issues to be resolved before we go forward are . . . ?
To expose unforeseen consequences	But won't your proposal have the effect of . . . ?

KEY POINTS

Questions are beneficial

- Encourage the audience to ask questions, as questions will add to your presentation
- A willingness to answer questions will enhance your credibility and keep the audience interested

Answer questions effectively

- Prepare answers to predictable questions
- Listen intently for any underlying meaning in the question
- Treat the questioner with respect, and try to refer back to your presentation when answering the question

Ask questions carefully

- A good question will prompt the recipient to consider a different angle or issue

CHAPTER SEVEN

CREATE A VIRTUOUS CYCLE

Only if you have been in the deepest valley can you ever know how magnificent it is to be on the highest mountain

RICHARD M. NIXON

When we won the World Debating Championship, a number of people told us that we were lucky. We agreed; after all, the decision in the final had been split six to five. But that wasn't what they meant. What they meant was: 'You are lucky to have been born knowing how to speak well'.

That is a popular fallacy that we have tried to debunk in previous chapters. Communicating effectively is not an inherited trait, it is about application. It is a skill that is learnt. Often when people see impressive speakers, they assume that it just comes naturally. We know that it does not. Before we won the World Debating Championship we also lost. On a number of occasions. In a number of countries and continents. Sometimes miserably. At first we used to leave these tournaments feeling angry. We couldn't understand why the judges seemed unable to recognise merit. But eventually we grew up. We learned to criticise ourselves and take criticism from others. We gained some self-insight.

The reason we eventually won was that we developed the ability to learn from our experiences. After every decision against us (even on the rare occasions where we disagreed with the result), we tried to understand what it was that made the judges *think that we had lost*.

We created a cycle of improvement. We gradually came to identify our strengths and weaknesses. We made an effort to capitalise on our strengths and eradicate our weaknesses. By the time we won, we were much better than we had been all those times when we lost. Some people think that analysing their own performance is easy. They give a speech to fifty people, five of their friends come up to them and say 'great job', so they naturally conclude that their communication was very effective.

They could be right, but it's also possible that they're being 'snowed'. After all, what is the likelihood that one of your friends will come up to you and say, 'Well, you really blew that one, didn't you?'. You need to be sure to take an objective look at your own performance. You need to ask yourself, 'How successful was that communication?' and, 'How could I have made it more successful?'.

If you are lucky enough to get some constructive criticism from a friend, colleague or member of the audience, don't be so arrogant as to argue with them or dismiss their criticism. Sometimes you will disagree with the points they raise, but their criticism will almost always be useful.

We know a number of people who speak well but are unlikely to improve as they are too arrogant and sensitive to criticism to accept any of the useful comments that people make regarding their performance. To become a highly effective communicator, you must be willing to make the effort to achieve constant improvement. The more effective you become, the less obvious will be the improvement, but that is just the law of diminishing returns.

Everyone has room to improve. It just takes a degree of self-analysis and a commitment to make it happen.

THE VIRTUOUS CYCLE

When you lack self-confidence, you perform badly. Because you perform badly, you lose even more self-confidence. It quickly becomes a vicious circle that is hard to break.

Few people, however, experience the *virtuous cycle*. The virtuous cycle works in much the same way as the vicious circle. As you improve, you become more self-confident. Your improved self-confidence makes you more successful, which makes you more confident, and so on.

The key to improving as a communicator is developing this virtuous cycle. Focus on your improvements and capitalise on them. In no time you will have developed a virtuous cycle and will be on the way to becoming a highly effective communicator.

Exhibit 7.1 *The virtuous cycle*

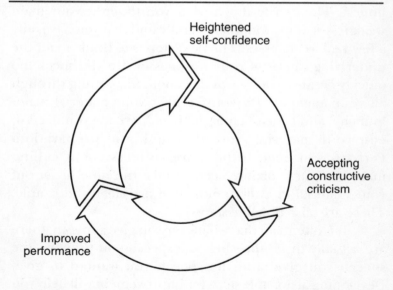

Heightened
self-confidence

Accepting
constructive
criticism

Improved
performance

Formulate actionable steps for improvement

After you have given a speech or presentation, or attended an interview, it is common to feel like kicking yourself — 'I know I could have done better', 'I spoke much too quickly and left out half of my best material', 'All my jokes went down like lead balloons', 'The audience was bored senseless'. Yet next time you go back and make all the same mistakes again. What you may not realise is that you have overcome the first great hurdle — you have recognised where you could improve, even though you haven't actually improved. At this stage you need to translate your weaknesses into actionable steps to improve your performance. Note that the steps must be *actionable*. There is no point in focusing on vague platitudes such as 'improve effectiveness', 'have greater impact' or 'develop a more powerful persona'.

After every significant communication, spend five minutes writing down what you thought you did well. Be honest. Then write down what you thought your main weaknesses were. You will generally find that you have only a few real weaknesses. The next step is to think about the underlying causes of your weaknesses. Do you speak too quickly because you're worried about not getting through all your material? Do you feel that your material is not 'punchy' and concise enough? If so, perhaps you need to edit your material more thoroughly in preparation. Perhaps you need to be more ruthless about culling material. You probably need to take the time to set out your material in bullet points that are clear and simple. These are all actionable steps.

It is often said that whenever you give a speech, there are actually three speeches: the speech you prepare, the speech you give, and the speech you wanted to give. Developing actionable steps for improvement will help you make the speech you give much closer to the speech that you wanted to give.

Take responsibility

Some speakers always assume that if their performance is poor, the fault lies with the audience. If people listening misunderstand a point or just don't get it, then there is a tendency to dismiss them. Often speakers take the view, 'Well, if they didn't get it then they're too stupid to worry about anyway'.

However, in any communication, a key element of your objective is that the audience understands what you are saying. If they don't, you should go back to the drawing board. Don't blame them.

CASE STUDIES

Below are extracts from three famous speeches: President Kennedy's inauguration speech, President Nixon's resignation speech, and Senator Edward Kennedy's withdrawal from the Presidential race in 1980.

They repay the time taken to read them as they illustrate some of the techniques that are often used by outstanding speakers to good effect.

We have not reproduced these extracts so that you can imitate the style or substance of these speeches. We have reproduced them for two reasons:

1. To demonstrate that you can and should learn from listening to effective communicators (reading their speeches is sometimes the next best alternative).
2. To show that even quite different styles can be highly effective.

Overall, Nixon's speech is certainly the least effective of the three. Given the circumstances in which it was made, it's understandable that he was not at his best. It is interesting because it clearly illustrates the dangers of not preparing at least an outline of your speech or presentation before making your remarks. Nixon was a highly effective speaker and this speech has moments of brilliance, but its main failing is that it has no coherent structure.

John F. Kennedy's speech is the most powerful of the three. It is emotionally charged. It strongly reinforces the feeling among the listening audience that they were present at a great moment in history, the beginning of a new era. When Kennedy said, 'the torch has been passed to a new generation . . . ' he indeed touched a generation of Americans.

Edward Kennedy's speech is extraordinary because, as a speech in defeat, it is powerful and triumphant. It is moving because of its powerful imagery, conveyed by the examples he uses to describe America's ills. Its power is further enhanced by the subconscious connection with his brothers and by the reference to them. The closing lines brilliantly convey an inspirational message.

John F. Kennedy, Inaugural Address, Washington DC, 1961

We observe today not a victory of party but a celebration of freedom, symbolising an end as well as a beginning, signifying renewal as well as change. For I have sworn before you and Almighty God the same solemn oath our forebears prescribed nearly a century and three-quarters ago.

The world is very different now. For man holds in his mortal hands the power to abolish all forms of human poverty and all forms of human life. And yet the same revolutionary belief for which our forbears fought is still at issue around the globe, the belief that the rights of man come not from the generosity of the state but from the hand of God.

We dare not forget today that we are the heirs of that first revolution. Let the words go forth from this time and place, to friend and foe alike, that the torch has been passed to a new generation of Americans, born in this country, tempered by war, disciplined by a hard and bitter peace, proud of our ancient heritage, and unwilling to witness or permit the slow undoing of these human rights to which this nation has always been committed, and to which we are committed today at home and around the world.

Let every nation know, whether it wishes us well or ill, that we shall pay any price, bear any burden, meet any hardship, support any friend, oppose any foe to assure the survival and the success of liberty . . . to those nations who would make themselves our adversary, we offer not a pledge but a request: that both sides begin anew the quest for peace, before the dark powers of destruction unleashed by science engulf all humanity in planned or accidental self-destruction.

We dare not tempt them with weakness. For only when our arms are sufficient beyond doubt can we be certain that they will never be employed.

But neither can two great and powerful groups of nations take comfort from our present course — both sides overburdened by the cost of modern weapons, both rightly alarmed by the spread of the deadly atom, yet both racing to alter that uncertain balance of terror that stays the hand of mankind's final war.

So let us begin anew, remembering on both sides that civility is not a sign of weakness, and sincerity is always subject to proof. Let us never negotiate out of fear, but let us never fear to negotiate.

Let both sides explore what problems unite us instead of belabouring those problems which divide us.

Let both sides, for the first time, formulate serious

and precise proposals for the inspection and control of arms, and bring the absolute power to destroy other nations under the absolute control of all nations.

Let both sides seek to involve the wonders of science instead of its terrors. Together let us explore the stars, conquer the deserts, eradicate disease, tap the ocean depths and encourage the arts and commerce.

Let both sides unite to heed in all corners of the earth the command of Isaiah to 'undo the heavy burdens . . . [and] let the oppressed go free'.

And if a beachhead of cooperation may push back the jungle of suspicion, let both sides join in creating a new endeavour, not a new balance of power, but a new world of law, where the strong are just and the weak secure and the peace preserved.

All this will not be finished in the first one hundred days. Nor will it be finished in the first one thousand days, nor in the life of this Administration, nor even perhaps in our lifetime on this planet. But let us begin.

In your hands, my fellow citizens, more than mine, will rest the final success or failure of our course. Since this country was founded, each generation of Americans has been summoned to give testimony to its national loyalty. The graves of young Americans who answered the call to service surround the globe.

Now the trumpet summons us again — not as a call to bear arms, though arms we need; not as a call to battle, though embattled we are; but a call to bear the burden of a long twilight struggle, year in and year out, 'rejoicing in hope, patient in tribulation', a struggle against the common enemies of man: tyranny, poverty, disease and war itself.

Can we forge against these enemies a grand and global alliance, North and South, East and West, that can assure a more fruitful life for all mankind? Will you join in that historic effort?

In the long history of the world, only a few generations have been granted the role of defending freedom in its hour of maximum danger. I do not shrink from this responsibility; I welcome it. I do not believe that any of us would exchange places with any other people or any other generation. The energy, the faith, the devotion which we bring to this endeavour will light our country and all who serve it, and the glow from that fire can truly light the world.

And so, my fellow Americans, ask not what your country can do for you; ask what you can do for your country.

My fellow citizens of the world, ask not what America will do for you, but what together we can do for the freedom of man.

Finally, whether you are citizens of America or citizens of the world, ask of us here the same high standards of strength and sacrifice which we ask of you. With a good conscience our only sure reward, with history the final judge of our deeds, let us go forth to lead the land we love, asking His blessing and His help, but knowing that here on earth God's work must truly be our own.

This speech is one of the most famous in history. It employs a number of useful techniques to motivate and inspire an audience. President Kennedy was very concerned to have a memorable inauguration. He asked his principal speech writer, Theodore Sorensen, to write a speech that would capture the essence of Lincoln's Gettysburg address. Kennedy even adopted Lincoln's cadences. He used an oratorical device that Lincoln was very fond of: starting sentences with the word 'let', giving a sense of higher authority.

Kennedy also used some linguistic devices that are

no longer in vogue, for instance the use of contrapuntalism, as in 'Let us never negotiate out of fear. But let us never fear to negotiate'. It is powerful oratory, but these days we tend to find it a little corny; we are reminded of old chestnuts like 'fail to plan — plan to fail'.

Kennedy's speech is outstanding, but it would be somewhat out of place coming from a world leader in the 1990s. Yet we still look back and remember that speech as inspirational.

Richard Nixon, 'Au revoir' speech, Washington DC, 1974

You are here to say goodbye to us, and we don't have a good word for it in English — the best is 'au revoir'. We will see you again . . .

Sure, we have done some things wrong in this Administration, and the top man always takes the responsibility, and I have never ducked it. But I want to say one thing: We can be proud of it — five and a half years. No man or no woman came into this Administration and left it with more of this world's goods than when he came in. No man or no woman ever profited at the public expense or public till. That tells something about you.

Mistakes, yes. But for personal gain, never. You did what you believed in. Sometimes right, sometimes wrong. And I only wish that I were a wealthy man — at the present time, I have got to find a way to pay my taxes — and if I were, I would like to recompense you for the sacrifices that all of you have made to serve in government.

But you are getting something in government — and I want you to tell this to your children, and I hope the Nation's children will hear it, too — something in government service that is far more important than money. It is a cause bigger than yourself. It is the cause of making this the greatest nation in the world, the leader of the world, because without our leadership, the world will know nothing but war, possibly starvation or worse, in the years ahead. With our leadership it will know peace, it will know plenty . . .

We think sometimes when things happen that don't go the right way; we think that when you don't pass the bar exam the first time — I happened to, but I was just lucky; I mean my writing was so poor the bar examiner said 'We have just got to let the guy through'. We think that when someone dear to us dies, we think that when we lose an election, we think that when we suffer a defeat, that all is ended.

Not true. It is only a beginning, always. The young must know it; the old must know it. It must always sustain us, because the greatness comes not when things go always good for you, but the greatness comes and you are really tested, when you take some knocks, some disappointments, when sadness comes, because only if you have been in the deepest valley can you ever know how magnificent it is to be on the highest mountain.

Like the curate's egg, this speech is good in parts. Nixon was speaking under extremely difficult circumstances. Facing imminent impeachment over the Watergate scandal, Nixon had that morning resigned the office of the Presidency of the United States. The 'au revoir' speech was an off-the-cuff talk that he gave to the White House staff who had gathered to say goodbye.

It reads like an impromptu speech, although the text does not adequately convey the emotion. It has obvious structural flaws. It is somewhat rambling. It moves from one point to another somewhat arbitrarily. At times it goes off on a tangent; the remarks about his bar exams, for instance, seem rather out of place.

Nixon, however, was a great orator and this speech has some classic Nixon techniques. He made his *mea culpas* but still managed to substantially deflect criticism to the last, for instance, 'Mistakes, yes. But for personal gain, never' or, 'Sure, we have done some things wrong in this Administration . . . but . . . we can be proud of it'.

The most effective line in this speech is the closing: 'only if you have been in the deepest valley can you ever know how magnificent it is to be on the highest mountain'. This conveys vividly the picture of Nixon's life — the highs of reaching the Presidency, and the lows of resignation.

Edward Kennedy, withdrawal speech at the Democratic convention, New York, 1980

There were hard hours on our journey, and often we sailed against the wind. But always we kept our rudder true, and there were so many of you who stayed the course and shared our hope. You gave your help; but even more, you gave your hearts.

Because of you, this has been a happy campaign. You welcomed Joan, me and our family into your homes and neighbourhoods, your churches, your campuses, your union halls. When I think back on all the miles and all the months and all the memories, I think of you. I recall the poet's words, and I say: What golden friends I have.

Among you, my golden friends across this land, I have listened and learned.

I have listened to Kenny Dubois, a glass blower in Charleston, West Virginia, who has ten children to support but has lost his job after thirty-five years, just three years short of qualifying for his pension . . .

I have listened to the grandmother in East Oakland

who no longer has a phone to call her grandchildren because she gave it up to pay the rent on her small apartment.

I have listened to young workers out of work, to students without the tuition for college, and to families without the chance to own a home. I have seen the closed factories and the stalled assembly lines of Anderson, Indiana and South Gate, California, and I have seen too many, far too many idle men and women desperate to work. I have seen too many, far too many working families desperate to protect the value of their wages from the ravages of inflation.

Yet I have also sensed a yearning for a new hope among the people in every state where I have been. And I have felt it in their handshakes, I saw it in their faces, and I shall never forget the mothers who carried children to our rallies. I shall always remember the elderly who have lived in an America of high purpose who believe that it can all happen again.

Tonight, in their name, I have come here to speak for them. And for their sake, I ask you to stand with them. On their behalf I ask you to restate and reaffirm the timeless truth of our party.

I congratulate President Carter on his victory here.

I am confident that the Democratic Party will reunite on the basis of Democratic principles, and that together we will march towards a Democratic victory in 1980.

And someday, long after this convention, long after the signs come down, and the crowds stop cheering, and the bands stop playing, may it be said of our campaign that we kept the faith. May it be said of our party in 1980 that we found our faith again.

And may it be said of us, both in dark passages and in bright days, in the words of Tennyson that my brothers quoted and loved, and that have special meaning for me now:

'I am a part of all that I have met
Tho' much is taken, much abides
That which we are, we are —
One equal temper of heroic hearts
   strong in will
To strive, to seek, to find, and not to yield.'

For me, a few hours ago, this campaign came to an end. For all those whose cares have been our concern, the work goes on, the cause endures, the hope still lives and the dream shall never die.

Senator Edward Kennedy's speech, like John F. Kennedy's inaugural address, was brilliantly effective. Certainly Carter's acceptance speech paled in comparison. The most memorable part of this speech is the ending: 'the work goes on, the cause endures, the hope still lives and the dream shall never die'. When those words were delivered in 1980, the effect was chilling; conjuring up images of hope and dreams as well as of John F. Kennedy and Robert F. Kennedy, both of whom were assassinated in the 1960s. This speech is brilliant because of the moving way it defends the Democratic ideals and the themes that Edward Kennedy and his brothers championed. Senator Kennedy's phrase 'may it be said of us' is a similar technique to John F. Kennedy's 'Let us . . . '. Generally, Edward Kennedy's speech is written in plain English and is far more down to earth than that of his brother's. This is partly a matter of context. After all, while John F. Kennedy's speech reflects the beginning a new era as President, Edward Kennedy was bowing out of the Presidential race.

What can you learn from these speeches?

These three speeches are captivating to listen to. Not just because of the words and emotion but also because of their place in history. They help us appreciate the power of speech and to understand that a diversity of styles can be highly effective. We hear people communicate all the time, every day. When you are impressed by someone's style of speech, take the time to work out what it is that has impressed you. Determine whether there is anything that they are doing that you can do too.

The trick is not to try to emulate someone else's style. That does not work. Everyone has their own style. Rather, work out what *techniques* you find effective. How are they getting the audience so involved? Why is their message so clear? Why is there such complete agreement? You can then adapt their techniques and apply them to your own communication.

LEARN FROM YOUR MISTAKES

If you hope to develop any skill, whether it is effective communication or a game like tennis, you need to know the theory, practise the activity and learn from your mistakes. This final element, learning from your mistakes, is not as easy as it sounds. It requires great honesty and patience.

When someone critiques your performance, your initial reaction may be to become defensive. You must learn to overcome this defensiveness so that you can learn from the wisdom of others. Be careful of the tendency to 'shoot the messenger'. If someone provides you with constructive criticism, don't let your reaction to the criticism manifest itself as hostility to the person who is only trying to help you improve.

The spoken word is a powerful tool. You can use it to help you achieve objectives in both your personal and your professional life. Remember that the basic principles for effective communication remain the same whether you are talking to your child's teacher or resigning the

Presidency. To make the most of your opportunities in life, you must be able to communicate effectively. We hope the seven steps outlined in this book will help you achieve this.

KEY POINTS

Create a virtuous cycle
- Build on your strengths
- Accept constructive criticism
- Be confident — it will boost your performance

Formulate actionable steps for improvement
- Be self-critical
- Work out what you could do today to communicate more effectively tomorrow

Learn by listening to others
- Understand that a range of styles can be effective
- Learn by listening to others, and adapting their techniques

---

BIBLIOGRAPHY

Aitken, Jonathon 1993, *Nixon: A Life*, Weidenfield & Nicolson, London.

Dixit, Avinash K. & Nalebuff, Barry J. 1991, *Thinking Strategically*, W.W. Norton & Co., New York.

MacKay, Hugh 1994, *Why Don't People Listen?*, Pan Macmillan, Sydney.

Marcus, Judy 1980, *Communication Dynamics*, Self published, Greenwich, US.

Philips, Jeremy & Hooke, James 1994, *The Debating Book*, University of New South Wales Press, Sydney.

Seinfeld, Jerry 1993, *SeinLanguage*, Bantam Books, Moorebank.

Sun Tzu, *The Art of War*, Hodder & Stoughton, Chatham, UK.

The Hamlyn Pocket Dictionary of Quotations 1979, ed. J. Hunt, Hamlyn, Sydney.

The Penguin Book of Twentieth Century Speeches 1992, ed. B. MacArthur, Viking, Ringwood.

The Penguin Dictionary of Modern Quotations 1980, 2nd edn, eds J.M. Coheny & M.J. Coheny, Penguin, London.

INDEX